THE
AI
FACTOR

THE
AI
FACTOR

How to Apply Artificial Intelligence and Use Big Data to Grow Your Business Exponentially

ASHA SAXENA

Post Hill
PRESS

A POST HILL PRESS BOOK

The AI Factor:
How to Apply Artificial Intelligence and Use Big Data to Grow Your
Business Exponentially
© 2023 by Asha Saxena
All Rights Reserved

ISBN: 978-1-63758-457-6
ISBN (eBook): 978-1-63758-458-3

Cover design by Tiffani Shea
Interior design and composition by Greg Johnson, Textbook Perfect

Post Hill Press
New York • Nashville
posthillpress.com

Published in the United States of America
4 5 6 7 8 9 10

*This book is dedicated to the mission and members
of Women Leaders in Data and AI (WLDA),
where we bring senior leaders together to create an
impactful digital world with parity and equity.*

*I founded WLDA in 2020 as an exclusive
peer-to-peer networking and mastermind group
for female and male leaders working together
for growth and sustainability.
These amazing people already have a seat
at the table and are making it possible
for many more to join them.*

Contents

Foreword

According to a recent PricewaterhouseCoopers (PwC) study, artificial intelligence will add more than fifteen trillion U.S. dollars to the global economy by 2030. Yet here we sit in 2022 with a recent study from Morning Consult showing that only 35 percent of organizations around the world have adopted AI in their enterprises. To hit the predicted mark by 2030, a much broader adoption of AI is required.

So, what's the missing link? This book has the answers to that question.

There are four things you must consider that are highly interrelated and dependent on one other—four "missing links," if you will. First, there must be a system of metrics demonstrating real business value—and no, the number of AI models built is not the right metric. AI should be tied to cost savings or new revenue. The second is having trust in the AI. For this to happen, it needs to be transparent, explainable, fair, robust, and it must preserve privacy. Third, the entire AI pipeline must have the ability to be truly observable throughout the enterprise. Finally, an AI strategy must be solidly tied to business strategy. By supplying these missing links, you can place humans at the center of AI outcomes and the overall value chain.

The human component is often missed in this context. Usually, when companies talk about human-centered AI, they are speaking more from a user experience perspective. Asha's book adds the perspective of the humans being impacted by the AI as well as the humans using it, which may or may not be the same person. She also brings in the humans in the business, a dimension I haven't included to date in my own thinking.

You can have the best strategy solidly tied to your AI plans, but if your business and by your customers don't adopt your plan, the ROI will be negative. Trust is critical to both. To truly address the pillars of trust I have defined through my experience, you need to take humans into account. This book will help you to do that in a highly effective and highly scalable manner.

What Asha describes in this book is a well thought-out and experience-based approach to building an AI strategy wholly based on one's business strategy. This unique perspective comes from someone who has had (and continues to have) a highly successful career in both data and business. Her "Data Power Canvas" helps lay the groundwork to address all four of the missing links identified above.

This book provides additional value: the ability to define where you are today on your journey and continually measure it in the "Power Quadrants for Data-Driven Companies." When using it as a precursor to the "Data Power Canvas," this will solve for the connection to business strategy.

The beauty of this book is the engaging approach taken to explain the value and execution of Asha's methodologies, through real-world examples of how companies such as Netflix and Starbucks have successfully implemented AI at a massive scale in their enterprise. She also cites lesser known, but equally significant, replicable examples from her own expert career and from those of other well-known experts in the industry.

If you want to be one of the companies capturing part of the over $15 trillion of GDP, then I suggest taking the time to read—and more importantly implement—the concepts in this book.

How much of that $15 trillion will *you* capture?

Dr. Seth Dobrin is IBM's first Global Chief AI Officer. In his role, Seth leads IBM's corporate AI strategy and is responsible for connecting the development and governance of AI across IBM's business units with a systemic creation of business value. The commitment to human-centered AI prompted Seth to create a new methodology helps companies develop AI strategies built on trust, providing business outcomes that are more fair, more accurate, and focused on the needs of real humans. This methodology has helped elevate AI from being simply a tool used to make processes more efficient to an overarching catalyst of business transformation. In 2021, Seth was recognized as AI Innovator of the Year at the AIconics Awards and was named one of Corinium's Top 100 Leaders in Data & Analytics.

Introduction

For the Oakland Athletics, the 1990s was a decade of mediocre results. Many blamed Oakland's inability to hire the best players, compared with major market teams like the Yankees. The reality was (and is) that teams with tons of TV revenue—like those in New York and LA—can always outspend teams like Oakland by two or even three to one.

In 2002, Oakland had one of the three lowest payrolls in Major League Baseball—light years behind the Yankees. Without the budget to hire top players, their prospects were dim. But general manager Billy Beane had a different approach. Using a statistical technique known as sabermetrics, his team defied conventional wisdom on individual player potential. They identified undervalued players based on non-traditional measurements—as opposed to scouts' gut feelings and over-simplified stats. Since the undervalued players were affordable, Beane reasoned, he could build a winning team on his tight budget.

Michael Lewis described this in his controversial book, *Moneyball*,[1] the basis for the 2011 film of that name. According to Lewis, Beane's unorthodox approach changed the game forever.

That year, the Athletics recorded an unprecedented twenty-game winning streak and made it to the playoffs that year and the next.

Since then, other teams—and other sports—have adopted a data-centric approach to the business of sports, harnessing data in ways that have multiplied their success. A *Forbes* writer noted that today's sports franchises now include three major new actors: big data, analytics, and artificial intelligence or AI.[2]

Why This Book?

Like so many others, you may be wondering if this is even possible for your organization. From Michael Lewis's book to Stanley Kubrick's classic movie, *2001*, to a long list of books and articles on AI, you already have some idea of its potential. But the questions are, "What can I actually *do* about it?" and "What makes this book different from other AI books?"

Before you read further, let me tell you why I felt the need to write this book. Yes, there are other volumes on the importance of AI, machine learning, predictive analytics, and other assorted data technologies. Some will even explain (as I have) the importance of executive buy-in, data literacy, and overall data readiness. But none of this addresses the unique cultural requirements that a coherent, consistent data strategy demands. This book covers the full gamut of why we need AI and how to get started as well as the framework and important elements needed for a successful implementation.

I was discussing this very thing with my colleague, Cameron Davies, Chief Data Officer for Yum! Brands and a trusted ally of Women Leaders in Data and AI (WLDA), the peer-to-peer mastermind community and mission-based networking organization I founded in 2020. As any friend would, he asked what was that unique *something* that would make this book stand out.

"Everybody talks about AI and organizational readiness from a technical perspective," he said. "They talk about it from a data perspective. But nobody talks about organizational readiness from a *cultural* perspective. Yes, we talk about how the culture needs to change, but we forget how the *existing* culture influences the way you even approach the problem."

He continued, "With a company like Virgin, CEO Branson simply says, 'I want this many AI projects in the next five years. You guys make it happen,' and it's an unquestioned mandate. But with other companies, the CEO may be on board with a data strategy, but there are four other executives, or four other divisions, or a board that aren't convinced—or have other priorities."

I knew the answer to Cameron's question. In this book, I had to do more than affirm conventional wisdom about big data and AI. I had to find a way to reach business and data leaders on a broad, practical, and cross-cultural level without oversimplifying. I had to find a model that, like Maslow's hierarchy of needs,[*] would stand on its own, and would help everyone visualize the concepts immediately. More important, it would give them a clear blueprint—a four-step process if you will—for making AI a practical reality.

To start, I decided to create my own AI-specific version of the classic "business model canvas" approach. Like the original, my version provides a *visual overview* of the building blocks required to plan and measure a successful strategy (including potential trade-offs) involving AI, machine learning, or predictive analytics. Its purpose is to guide a strategy that will, I hope, be self-evident to everyone.

Having made such a bold statement, I invite you to continue reading to see how AI and big data can accomplish things you never imagined before.

---

[*] For the very few people who need a quick refresher on this concept, I recommend Dr. Saul McLeod's excellent summary: simplypsychology.org/maslow.html.

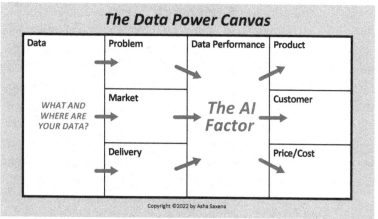

This chart is used and explained further in chapters 7 and 8.

My Own Journey

I began my data journey over twenty-five years ago. After starting as a computer science engineer, I became a tech entrepreneur, building a large data management consulting firm, an ecommerce company, and a healthcare analytics software firm. Under the auspices of CXO Coaching, CEO Coaching International, and WLDA, I have advised business leaders seeking to make business sense of these often confusing technologies.

Needless to say, I have always been fascinated by data, computer engineering, and the math itself. In the early days of my consulting career, I saw that the focus of many companies was on optimizing relational databases—*structured* data. "Let's get everything into the data warehouse," they said, "so we can generate reports that make sense." Now, the conversation has changed radically. The big data revolution has enabled us with the possibilities of using and processing both structured and unstructured data to deeply understand our consumers, our environment, and more.

For businesses, the data dilemma has become acute thanks to the "three v's" of big data, which we'll explore in chapter 2. The sheer *volume* of data has increased exponentially into petabyte territory[3] and beyond. Thanks to ever-faster processors and connections, its speed or *velocity* is approaching that of instantaneous real-time access. The third "v," *variety*, is the most challenging of all. This ocean of data is now predominantly *unstructured*, consisting of conversations, images, audio, video, and other forms that defy traditional data models. It's no wonder business leaders struggle to find that "fourth v" inherent in big data: *value*.

Much later, as my career progressed from data science to the business world, I began to notice something significant. Stepping outside my scientific circle, I found that business leaders and executives knew they needed data but did not know how to find it or what to do with what they had. (To be fair, data scientists often have the opposite problem. They know how to work with the data but do not always see its full business potential.)

The truth is that many, if not most, business leaders already have the data potential to achieve dramatic success. The problem is they don't know how to find or use it. As this book will show, the only way to effectively identify, collect, and leverage big data is through the use of artificial intelligence or AI. These are digital technologies that mimic the problem-solving and decision-making capabilities of the human mind—detecting patterns and solving routine problems with more accuracy and greater speed than humans alone could ever handle. The AI Factor is not the sole domain of big and powerful companies; you can use it too.

•———•

Of the many misconceptions about AI and its related technology, the most pernicious is the notion that only huge, sophisticated entities can use them—and that their use is in some way unethical or irresponsible. The media typically magnifies this image of big tech dominating big data, leading to a feeling of hopelessness among ordinary business leaders. For example, the "big three" tech companies (Google, Facebook, and Amazon) dominate digital ad spending as of this writing, thanks to their use of AI and customer data to predict consumer behavior. But their continued dominance is by no means assured, as privacy concerns about the use of customer data are likely to cause a damaging backlash.[4] Such a gloomy news narrative distracts us from the fact that other companies are benefitting from predictive and behavior analytics and are doing so in a more responsible and sustainable manner.

Why Data and AI Matter

This book is about you and your business—and the hidden potential of your data. Like the Oakland Athletics, you are struggling with outsized, seemingly immovable internal and external limitations. But like Billy Beane, you have potential access to data that can unlock a different outcome. (Or you may already have the data but don't know what to do with it.) And unlike the world of 2002, you now have far greater access to AI and other forces that can leverage big data in new and dramatic ways to propel your business or association to new levels of success. It may seem strange and unfamiliar, but all it takes is your decision to use these forces wisely.

Others in your business may be under the impression that AI is something strange or mysterious. So try this experiment. Ask if they've used artificial intelligence that day. Their most likely answer, after the puzzled look, will be no. If you press them, you'll find they don't know much about it. AI is something they've heard of in a movie or on TV. It's out there, but it doesn't really affect their daily lives. Perhaps you share that impression, but nothing could be further from the truth.

If you use a personalized banking app on your smartphone, then you're using AI. It guards your account against suspicious activity, uses your phone's camera to make check deposits, and recommends spending and investment options based on your activity and preferences. If you shop online, you're using AI, which recommends items and options that fit your browsing and buying behavior. If you use an online dating app, AI is using all that profile data to select a compatible prospect. Modern healthcare is increasingly driven by AI, which examines data patterns from often fragmented sources to provide faster, clearer information to providers and patients. Even some car insurance companies now use AI to monitor and reward safe driving behavior. In short, AI is everywhere.

You not only use AI many times a day, every day, but you also use—and benefit from—the *essential components* of AI, including big data, the cloud, smart devices, and more. This book is about all these forces, which are already becoming an integral, even essential part of our lives, whether we know it or not. Just as these technologies benefit individual consumers, they can also multiply the success of companies who use them well. This book is a road-map to such growth.

•———•

In the past, resistance to AI was understandable, but businesses cannot ignore it anymore. Big data and AI are now the critical path to growth despite the way they are portrayed in the media. Even now, the media portrays it in an overly sensational manner, as in the case of Replika,[5] an AI-driven chatbot app that allows users to create their own virtual friend. Some commentators pointed to its benevolent uses, such as giving disenfranchised people an outlet for judgment-free expression, but others voiced ethical and privacy concerns.[6] More recently, media outlets have treated the topic with alarm, citing the increased use of AI and facial recognition for oppressive political purposes.[7]

At times, it has also been a very public source of embarrassment, as Microsoft learned with its ill-fated chatbot, Tay, originally created as a conversational AI.[8] The company tried to create a cool, millennial-seeming persona on social media, based on AI processing of all its followers' posts. Predictably, it was PR disaster. The data set included a flood of deliberate posts by internet trolls. As a result, Tay's character rapidly devolved into a narrow, racist caricature. Technically, *the AI worked* but, thanks to the skewed data, not in the way its creators intended. Had Microsoft adhered more closely to the four basic "pillars" of *responsible AI* (organizational, operational, technical, and reputational),[9] the disaster may well have been averted. We'll discuss these more thoroughly in chapter 4.

The problem is that these stories—even the truthful ones—feed our common misperceptions about AI and big data. Such views are magnified further in movies and television, as we'll address in greater detail in chapter 2. As a result, we suffer from an unconscious bias that will damage our prospects in the long run. Whether as individuals or as business owners, we say "AI is too big, too scary, and too complicated for me." Then we add, "Only big companies like Amazon and Facebook can use AI and big data." Sometimes we infer that AI is too intrusive or even inherently unethical. But none of that is true, as we will see. In fact, as more companies and nonprofits learn to use these technologies in a responsible manner, they'll discover that the resulting growth in value and influence is not only impressive in a purely business sense, but also beneficial and ultimately *sustainable*.

The Four-Step Process

Like any respectable author, I'll do my best to give you a capsule summary of the basics here—so you can hold your own when a fellow executive or coworker wants to discuss it. But if you're impatient to get moving and really embrace the principles described in this volume, you're welcome to skip ahead to chapter 1.

Part one of this book begins with two "household name" companies—Netflix and Starbucks—that embody many of the data strategies that can multiply business growth. The second chapter lays out the concepts themselves, separating the myths about artificial intelligence from the actual science, and providing a clearer understanding of the potential each technology represents. In chapter 3, we will review an array of business types—each one different in purpose and structure but all benefiting from the AI Factor today.

The immense power of these forces cannot be underestimated. In chapter 4, we will outline what it means to use them ethically and responsibly. Recent events have proven that this technology, much more than all disruptive technologies before it, can produce results far more rapidly than our existing laws and traditions can manage. This means that the *responsible* use of big data and AI will result in *sustainable growth*—not only for individual companies and organizations like yours, but also for our body politic and the planet itself.

Part two of this book is where we explore the 'how,' following the principles I have used to advise business leaders for years. It provides a plan for realizing the benefits of AI and big data, no matter the type or size of your business or nonprofit. This is a four-step process:

- *Assessing your business*—In order to leverage these forces, the first step is to discover what type or stage of business you presently occupy based on your growth potential (real or perceived) and your willingness to innovate and take risks. Chapter 5 will help clarify these stages for you. For example, some companies are primarily looking to cut costs, optimize operational processes, and employ other defensive tactics. Others are in growth mode, pursuing mergers and acquisitions or looking to capture new market share. Still others are aggressively researching, designing, testing new products and services, and pursuing the talent needed to create them. Finally, some are looking to bend or break the rules—discarding everything to transform their business for exponential growth.

Whatever stage you are in, it's okay to understand and align with your business needs and goals. An honest assessment will not prevent you from implementing big data and AI. Rather, it will inform you *how* to do so more effectively. Regardless of what type of entity you lead, the AI Factor will enable you to succeed—either to evolve into a greater, more innovative business or simply become stronger in the stage you are in now.

- *Knowing your data-readiness framework*—The next step of the process—and the subject of chapter 6—is understanding and defining your business' structural organization and its readiness to pursue a data strategy. Your present ability to leverage AI and big data must be based on an honest assessment of your objectives, data management practices, and other factors that make up your data readiness. This will clearly demonstrate which of these areas need further development or even radical revision. These include actions you can take in areas such as organizational structure, data usage, strategic product planning, human resources, research and development (R&D), leadership practices, and customer service.

- *Prioritizing the first project*—The third step—and the subject of chapter 7—is to choose the business goal that not only can be enhanced by the AI Factor but also represents the greatest value. No company, not even Netflix or Starbucks, can simultaneously implement an AI strategy over multiple profit or cost centers. Prioritizing the highest value opportunity to utilize AI and big data will accomplish two things. First, it will let you assign resources to achieve a specific, measurable goal, with a high probability of beneficial results. Second, once successful, the AI expertise acquired and used to accomplish the first goal will inform the strategy for tackling the second, and so on. It will help dispel the fear and misconceptions surrounding AI, and inspire confidence in a responsible data-centric approach to business.

Chapter 7 will also cover many practical facets of the transformation needed to leverage big data and AI, including answering questions on your business model and the numbers behind your operations. It also asks probing questions about your competition and industry norms or conventions that may be unconsciously guiding your actions. In every case, benefiting from the AI Factor is a process grounded in a practical, realistic understanding of data science—something within the scope of any business.

- *Implement, measure, and scale*—In chapter 8, we'll cover the practical aspects of implementing the AI Factor, measuring the results, and guarding against unconscious assumptions or bias. We'll also cover the different criteria for measurement and action, which include important differences for product development, customer acquisition, and altering pricing and cost structures. The chapter will also address the all-important matter of scaling initial data projects to other and larger opportunities, potentially transforming your business or nonprofit beyond all expectations.

Of course, AI includes many other technologies and exciting new trends that fall outside the scope of this book. Chapter

9 serves not only to summarize the basic steps covered here but also to give you a glimpse of what's coming next. AI is but a precursor to the move toward data independence, advanced biometric devices, and what we have dubbed (for now) the metaverse and interaction via virtual reality interfaces. Like AI, these new technologies are subject to misconceptions and even abuse by short-sighted individuals and companies. But also like AI, they hold great promise for a better future.

The AI Factor includes technologies with obvious areas of overlap. The terminology can be confusing at times, so, to better understand the bigger picture, a glossary can be found at the end of the book, along with some recommended sources of information to help along the way.

•———•

These technologies affect every aspect of our business and personal life, whether we realize it or not. The purpose of this book is to show business leaders how they can understand, adapt, and utilize them to produce extreme growth in their own companies and organizations. It is also meant to help technology leaders understand how to apply their data in meaningful ways and multiply their companies' long-term value.

Each aspect of the AI Factor—individually and collectively—has the potential to address the inefficiencies and unmet needs that we must face in order to succeed. Using these principles as a framework, business leaders and technical professionals alike can uncover the enormous value of their data and use it to create lasting business impact.

I wish you every success in this exciting journey.

PART ONE

UNDERSTANDING THE AI FACTOR

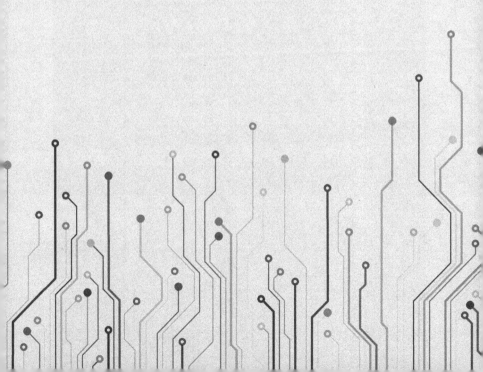

CHAPTER 1

How Netflix and Starbucks Changed the World

To change the world, you must always begin with what you *can* control—namely, your own personal or organizational decisions. This is a book about doing just that. By the time you finish reading, you'll have a basic roadmap for applying a very specific technology to those decisions. "The AI Factor" is the shorthand name I have given to artificial intelligence technology and its related components. As many before you have discovered, you will gain a practical understanding of its potential for exponential growth. But to fully appreciate what that means, let's look at some notable examples.

We'll start with two of the most recognizable brands on the planet: Netflix and Starbucks. When they first launched, neither company was a business superstar. They both had entered heavily saturated markets, with video stores and coffee shops on almost every corner in America. Both companies had collected data to improve business outcomes with relatively modest success.

But at one point, both companies did something different. They deliberately chose not only to gather vast quantities of data but to apply it in a truly scientific manner. By applying AI and big data, both companies created a quantitatively superior inflection point. As a result, their businesses multiplied in value.

> *Author's Note:* As I write this, both Netflix and Starbucks are going through a period of turmoil and uncertainty. But even though both companies are having hard times (as we all do), their long-term success is extremely likely. Analysts project that both Netflix[1] and Starbucks[2] will have continued, sustained growth over the long term—precisely *because* of their commitment to AI.

To be perfectly clear, *every* business can be a data-driven business if they use data and AI to grow or differentiate themselves from the competition. AI is not something that can only be used effectively by bigger companies with more data, financial resources, and technical people. The good news is that anyone can use data science to reach such an inflection point and multiply their business.

David and Goliath Revisited

In 1980s and '90s, Blockbuster was a household name. Friday nights were movie nights. My friends and I would roam up and down the aisles of tapes or DVDs, marveling at the terrible direct-to-video features and bemoaning that all the hot new releases had already been rented. Eventually, we would settle on a few films, grab some oversized boxes of junk food, scan the barcode on that infamous blue-and-gold Blockbuster card, and be off to watch movies and eat microwave popcorn. It was a comforting, familiar, and predictable experience.

However, the Blockbuster business model also came with downsides for its customers. It was inconvenient, choices were limited, and there were the infamous late charges that would accrue if you were even one day late returning a movie. (According to *Quartz*,[3] late charges produced 16 percent of the company's revenue.) In spite of it all, Blockbuster dominated the movie rental landscape. By 1994, when Viacom bought the company for $8.4 billion, Blockbuster Video had more than 6,000 stores and went public five years later.

But by 2010, Blockbuster had filed for bankruptcy. Dish Network purchased the company in 2012. But in 2013, it announced it would be closing all remaining stores. As of this writing, Blockbuster Video survives solely in the form of a single store in Bend, Oregon,[4] that has been turned into an Airbnb.

What happened?

You may already know the big plot points of the story. In 2000, Netflix founders Reed Hastings and Marc Randolph offered to sell their company to Blockbuster for $50 million and Blockbuster shortsightedly said "No, thanks." But you may not be as familiar with the true reason that, just thirteen years after its founding, Netflix was able to overtake and eventually crush the seemingly unbeatable Blockbuster.

Popular mythology holds that Blockbuster's leadership squandered its huge advantage in the marketplace by becoming complacent, failing to recognize the internet's disruptive potential. They fell hopelessly behind Netflix and rival Redbox in the race to innovate, implementing scattershot, ineffective programs in a panicked attempt to remain relevant. To some degree, that is true. Blockbuster's unwillingness to change made them a willing accomplice in their own demise.

But Netflix did much more than sit back and watch their chief adversary self-destruct. They were eager to change—breaking and remaking their business model every few years. They made strategic decisions that enabled them to leap past Blockbuster faster than anyone thought possible. Those decisions were based on data. But first, a short case study.

That Little Mail-Order DVD Rental Company

Netflix was the brainchild of Hastings and Randolph, who admired the ecommerce success of Amazon. It launched in 1997 with thirty employees and a movie library of 925 titles. They intended to leverage Hastings's computer science background and Randolph's mail-order experience to challenge the leading players in the $15 billion home video rental industry. Netflix was not a streaming company in its early days. The bandwidth that would allow real-time streaming of high-quality video content was not yet commercially available.

It those early years, Netflix was a mail-order DVD rental company not unlike Blockbuster in some ways. Customers requested a DVD via the website, paid a rental fee, and the DVD would be mailed to them. Customers would also create their "queue" on the Netflix website, reserving their virtual place in line to rent the movies they wanted to see on a first-come, first-served basis. After Netflix instituted a flat monthly subscription fee in the early 2000s, the company went public in 2002 and turned a profit by 2003.

However, the choices that would change everything about home entertainment and original content creation and distribution began in 2002. Hastings and his team knew that players like Walmart and Amazon—companies with far more capital resources than Netflix—were talking about making their own forays into the home video market. They knew that for all its popularity, Netflix's original value proposition was built on a few key but *non-exclusive* points: the convenience of home delivery, unlimited movie rentals, and no due dates or late fees. These would be incredibly easy for a larger, better-funded rival to replicate, allowing them to steal a huge fraction of Netflix's customers. In order to stave off the competition and continue to grow, Netflix needed to disrupt their own business model and innovate.

Hastings revealed his thought process for the first time publicly in a 2002 interview with *Wired* magazine.[5] In it, he said, "The dream twenty years from now [is] to have a global entertainment distribution company that provides a unique channel for film studios and producers." Hastings knew that when download speeds finally became high enough to allow real-time streaming, that same capability would be available to everyone, making it just as replicable as Netflix's mail-order business.

But what could no other competitor copy? Exceptional original programming from the best writers, producers, directors, and performers in the world. If Netflix could become the leading conduit for that content, it would dominate. At Netflix, the long-term vision was to "become HBO faster than HBO can become us."[6]

The process began with Netflix's CineMatch system. After a customer rated twenty films on a five-star scale, the algorithm would take this and other data—including the customer's rental history, ratings by other customers, and key metadata about the movies themselves—and identify patterns in order to predict similar movies that the customer might want to rent in the future. The algorithm also used this data to suggest movies to customers with similar profiles. Netflix shared the data with movie studios to help them plan their marketing campaigns. Netflix was doing what everyone must do if they wish to grow exponentially:

Use data to get to know their customers better than they know themselves.

It did not stop there. In 2006, Netflix made news around the world by launching the Netflix Prize.[7] The company would pay $1 million to the first person or programming team to create an algorithm that would be more accurate at recommending movies based on the personal preferences of Netflix customers. The company gave competitors a data set that included more than one hundred million user movie ratings, and in 2009, a seven-member team called BellKor's Pragmatic Chaos delivered the winning algorithm, which beat the accuracy of CineMatch's recommendations by 10 percent.

The Netflix Prize was the next move in the company's game of chess toward its ultimate goal as a content distribution platform. The end goal of the upgraded algorithm was not to recommend a better selection of romantic comedies for Saturday date night, but to give Netflix the ability to gather ever more precise, comprehensive data about its customers' preferences and tastes in entertainment. The company was building a powerful data infrastructure that was to become the key to its extraordinary growth.

Streaming

In 2005, Hastings saw that online streaming would become the future of home entertainment. In January 2007, the technology caught up to his vision—sort of. Netflix announced that it would be rolling out its video-on-demand service with 1,000 available titles. However, broadband was still in its infancy, and the service was a compliment to the DVD mail-order service, not a replacement.

Streaming content quickly became Netflix's signature, especially as broadband connectivity and servers became much faster. Although it was still mailing DVDs, (as it still does, to about two million customers annually in 2020),[8] the company transitioned to making its entire catalog available via streaming. People loved the convenience of being able to stay at home on the couch and choose from tens of thousands of ever-changing programs. However, around 2010, increased bandwidth also led to competition from brands like Hulu and Amazon Prime.

This is where Hastings's vision and investments in data and AI paid off. He and Netflix's leadership knew if they were to gain an edge over competitors like Hulu and Amazon, they could not simply be conduits of other people's content but creators of *original* content. Netflix's massive subscriber database didn't just give the platform the power to popularize films and TV programs by targeting them to specific users, it also would allow Netflix to partner with filmmakers to create content specifically tailored to the tastes of its subscribers.

Filmmakers would gain a dedicated distribution and marketing channel and avoid the task of getting their movies into theaters. Netflix would gain a pipeline of original content. After all, with a big enough budget, any company could create its own streaming service. But without Netflix's focus on big data and AI, no one would easily create original shows like *Orange is the New Black* or *Stranger Things*.

Data-Driven Innovation

So began Netflix's era of data-driven innovation. It was a giant bet, and it paid even bigger dividends. In 2018 Netflix invested about $13 billion in content, most of it on original shows. David Fincher's series *House of Cards* debuted in 2013, followed by many more, including *Bird Box* (watched by forty-five million households on its debut weekend), *Unbreakable Kimmy Schmidt*, *Ozark*, *Bojack Horseman*, and many more. As Blake Morgan wrote in *Forbes*, "Original content is what stands out to viewers. They can watch most network shows in multiple places, but they can only get original content straight from Netflix."

That flow of top-quality original content—shaped and informed by terabytes of precise data on customer likes and dislikes—has made Netflix the colossus of the home entertainment landscape: $20 billion in revenue, $2.6 billion in profits, more than 195 million subscribers through 3Q of 2020, and about 9,000 employees. Most important, the company has reshaped its industry in a way few companies ever do.

In 2016, Netflix started releasing entire seasons of new shows at once, once again disrupting the industry. This was a powerful differentiating value proposition over cable, as is the fact that, as of this writing,* Netflix doesn't run advertising. They were the first company in the space to enable mobile viewing via smart phones, tablets, and other devices, even making their programming available over the typical smartphone's data network. Netflix's stellar growth has also spun off new competitors. Streaming services are everywhere, and many are also producing their own original content. While the debate rages over who is number one at the moment, Netflix still retains the long-term advantage.

The company's new value propositions are largely non-replicable because they are built on Netflix's massive store of unique subscriber preference data. Streaming competitors can produce their own content, but they can't duplicate Netflix's deep years-long knowledge of what its customers like and care about.

In part two of the book, we will explore in detail the steps necessary to leverage AI and big data successfully—no matter what size your business or nonprofit may be. But if you'll be patient a while longer, let's break down the roadmap that Netflix provides:

- Company executives were fully aware of their business posture—both in terms of growth potential and their willingness to take risks. Entering a crowded market with a dominant competitor, they were more interested in **disrupting existing business models** than cutting costs and optimizing existing processes.

---

* Recently, in response to revenue declines attributed to password-sharing and other factors, Netflix has proposed a lower-cost, "lite" version of its subscription service, which would be supported by advertising revenue.

- From the start, the company was acutely aware of the importance of their existing data and took steps to **constantly improve their data readiness** and use data to improve their value proposition. This included creating new ways to gather even more data and exploit its potential business value.

- They deliberately **prioritized data strategies and projects** that represented not only the predictive value of the data but also the project's business value. Specifically, they developed and improved the accuracy of their predictive analytics algorithms for customer behavior.

- During this process, and in its subsequent iterations of their data and AI strategy, the company measured the results and used them to scale its business, rather than simply improving its existing services. It used its data advantage to **open entirely new business opportunities**. This included new content creation that would differentiate the company from other streaming services—and spawn numerous imitators.

Now, Netflix is even threatening the traditional cinema business model. When the COVID-19 pandemic forced the closure of movie theaters, audiences became even more accustomed to watching movies from home. Netflix, ever the disruptor, did its part with a Google Chrome extension called Netflix Party, which lets users share their real-time movie watching via live group chat and text. Even as traditional theater chains fight their way back, movie studios are hedging their bets by releasing feature films in theaters *and* streaming platforms, with little or no time in between. The pandemic also accelerated this strategy, as Netflix and its competitors gathered even more customer behavior data to predict their next business move.

Netflix was able to make all these bold bets in part because they relied on accruing and analyzing enormous amounts of customer data. By relying on objective data, not guesswork or wishful thinking, they mitigated a great deal of the risk involved in costly initiatives like spending billions of dollars on original content. Data drove everything from changes to the recommendation engine to partnerships with Hollywood, and Netflix simply followed the data to its new business model, like following a treasure map.

The result is a data-powered "virtuous cycle" that promises to keep the company's revenues growing and keep it ahead of streaming players. A continuous stream of original programming feeds the Netflix algorithm and AI nonstop with fresh data on subscriber likes and dislikes. By analyzing that data, the company gains insights that will drive the development of even more original programming, inspire new programs, encourage highly targeted programming for specific audiences, and stay ahead of the competition.

From Cars to Flying Cars

Netflix's secret sauce in gaining that deep knowledge was its optimized CineMatch recommendation algorithm. An algorithm is a clearly defined sequence of instructions that a computer uses to solve a specific problem or perform certain computations. While an algorithm is not exactly AI, the two are closely related. QuiGig founder Mir Mousavi described the relationship between algorithms and AI as the relationship between cars and flying cars. "The key difference," he says, "is that an algorithm defines the process through which a decision is made, and AI uses training data to make such a decision."[9]

Netflix uses different technologies to get the most predictive power from its massive database. First, its algorithm scours the Netflix database to find people who have rated the same movie similarly. For example, it might identify all customers who have given the Matt Damon vehicle *The Martian* a five-star rating. Then, the algorithm determines if those people have also rated a second movie...say, *Good Will Hunting*. The system will then calculate the likelihood that customers who liked *The Martian* will also like *Good Will Hunting*. If the statistical odds are high, the system will recommend *Good Will Hunting* to those other customers. This process will repeat millions of times, drawing an endless series of correlations between films and customers.

Netflix also relies on the *machine learning* aspect of AI. Rather than analyzing traditional *structured* data (names, phone numbers, email addresses, and the like), their AI examined *unstructured data*—namely images—which is far more subjective and difficult to categorize. In 2014, Netflix started examining the connection between the thumbnail images that users see on their Netflix home screens and which content they choose to watch. They found a strong correlation between the appeal of the thumbnails and the popularity of a TV show or movie.

The company started using machine learning to automatically generate multiple thumbnail images for each one of its shows and constantly test them against each other with its users. This is a classic "A/B test" scenario, where ten Netflix customers might see ten completely different sets of images *for the same movies or TV shows*, each one generated by AI. As they choose what to watch, the system logs those choices and changed its thumbnails to become more and more appealing. The company then uses AI to analyze the unstructured data from images and uses the results to guide its business strategy.

Not only have Netflix's recommendation engine and AI given independent films and filmmakers and out-of-the-mainstream content much greater visibility, but according to Blake Morgan in *Forbes*, the resulting deluge of high-quality original content has changed how people consume entertainment. Pre-Netflix, people consumed TV series and limited series slowly, one week at a time, so the impact of new shows was muted. Now, in what's been labeled "The Netflix Effect," people binge-watch entire seasons of new shows in a single day, creating culture-shaping hits and new TV and movie stars overnight.[10]

The Corner Coffee Shop

Before concluding that Netflix and its use of data and AI are business anomalies, let's consider another example: the ubiquitous Starbucks franchise. Originally founded in 1971 as a Seattle coffee roaster and reseller, the company grew steadily—and began selling espresso drinks directly in the 1980s, under the leadership of Howard Schultz. By expanding to new locations—many through acquisition of rival companies—the company had achieved enough success to go public in 1992.

In the early 2000s, Starbucks had its share of ups and downs, including setbacks in some international markets,[11] and the fallout from the 2007–2009 recession.[12] But it remained in a strong position. Like Netflix, the company goals and business strategy fostered a mentality of change—of becoming more than a commodity-only entity. And also, like Netflix, they could only do so by using data and AI.

In 2009, Starbucks launched its first smartphone app—originally a convenient, in-store payment app—in sixteen of its retail locations.[13] Over time, the company integrated its Starbucks Rewards program into the app, which had more than seventeen million active users by 2017, colleting customer purchase and preference data from more than ninety million transactions per week.[14] The company now uses that enormous data trove to personalize (and upsell) customer orders.[15] They also deploy the data in their personalized marketing campaigns and combine it with data on local demographics and traffic patterns in order to select locations for new stores. In other words:

Starbucks is not a coffee company;
it's a data company that sells coffee.[16]

Today, Starbucks is using big data and predictive analytics not only to personalize their customers' experience but also to dramatically increase company revenues by 21 percent annually.[17] In a 2018 survey by *The Manifest*,[18] the Starbucks mobile app was found to be the most regularly used loyalty app (48 percent of respondents) of major restaurant apps. Its integrated online ordering and loyalty program represented 39 percent of sales for the entire chain.[19] As we will see later in the chapter, this has a significant impact on the company's stock price.

The company continues to leverage technology to multiply their business. They also use artificial intelligence to create a "virtual barista" that can take orders via voice recognition,[20] and to remotely monitor its enormous array of critical, internet-enabled equipment—predicting when it will need repair or maintenance.[21]

As we will see, both Starbucks and Netflix achieved exponential results through their bold use of artificial intelligence, big data, intelligent devices, and the cloud. They changed how the world views AI. However, they are not alone. Other companies—of almost any size—can still benefit from this technology.

The Four Quadrants

To understand *how* a business can best apply AI and big data, one must first know their own willingness to take risks, tear down existing business models, and reinvent new ones. One must also be in a market with actual growth potential, whether it is fully known or not, as shown in the illustration on the following page.

Each quadrant represents a path forward in which big data and AI are the critical elements. Virtually any business will find a relevant goal in one of these quadrants depending on where it is in its life cycle, its current state of profitability, and other variables. For example, if your company is not currently positioned to take a leap like Netflix or Starbucks did, then it can almost certainly benefit from adopting an *optimizer* strategy, in which data

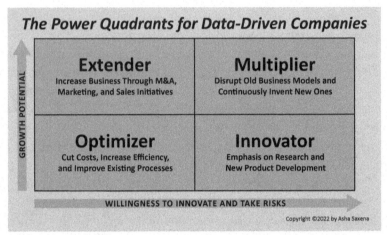

The Power Quadrants for Data-Driven Companies

Extender	**Multiplier**
Increase Business Through M&A, Marketing, and Sales Initiatives	Disrupt Old Business Models and Continuously Invent New Ones
Optimizer	**Innovator**
Cut Costs, Increase Efficiency, and Improve Existing Processes	Emphasis on Research and New Product Development

GROWTH POTENTIAL

WILLINGNESS TO INNOVATE AND TAKE RISKS

Copyright ©2022 by Asha Saxena

In a variation on classic business positioning, every type of business, no matter its inherent potential for growth or innovation, can benefit from the right use of AI and big data.

is collected and examined in order to find ways to increase efficiencies, lower costs, and upgrade product quality and customer service. For example, a company might use its store of internal data to optimize supply chain processes and lower costs.

If your current market growth potential is limited but you are willing to take more risks and innovate, then you could choose to pursue the *contender* strategy. You would invest in R&D and engineering in order to develop new products and services that might power a more aggressive initiative in the future. That's what Apple did when it invested years developing the first iPod, which launched the iOS ecosystem that in turn launched the global mobile economy.

Or perhaps a better fit would be the *extender* strategy, in which you leverage your data to drive the development of new marketing initiatives that attract new customers so you can grow your market share, spin off new brands or brand extensions, or grow your business through mergers and acquisitions.

These are all viable strategic choices for businesses that aspire to a *multiplier* strategy—like that of Netflix or Starbucks—but whose leadership, culture, or investors aren't ready to make such a commitment. Think of the optimizer, contender, and extender strategies as steps toward the ideal of becoming a multiplier business. As the benefits of AI and big data become apparent, the idea of adapting and evolving one's business through AI will become more apparent.

Following a multiplier strategy is not easy. In fact, it's often terrifying to a company's stakeholders because it appears as though you are taking your company out of safe harbor, where revenues and profits are predictable, and into unknown territory. However, sooner or later, all businesses must innovate and adapt in order to survive.

You may not be able to start with disrupting old business models right away, but you can still use AI now to aggressively increase efficiencies, develop new products, and grow through mergers and acquisitions (M&A). But in the end, the only proven way for your business to remain viable—especially in the volatile tech sector—will be to create a unique value proposition, one that your competitors can't easily replicate and improve upon. By doing so, you create a "flywheel effect" that channels the momentum of each data-driven decision into new insights and strategies for growth, as we'll discuss in chapter 8.

That means making a leap. That means innovating and even challenging your current business model in favor of one driven by AI and its related technologies.

Results of the Multiplier Mindset

Both Netflix and Starbucks are examples of multiplier businesses. As a leader, you need to have a vision. You need to think and dream big, but then you have to put a stake in the ground and have actual plans to make your dream a reality. True entrepreneurs are willing to take risks, but they also do tons of homework beforehand. They calculate all the risks before they launch a business and find ways to mitigate everything they can. When it came to the use of data and AI to predict outcomes, Netflix did exactly that, and the results were extraordinary.

After each company began pursuing strategies involving AI and big data, the value of their respective companies changed from being merely good to being exponentially greater. For example, the stock share price of Netflix has risen precipitously since they began applying these principles.

This growth is the reason why Netflix is now in the S&P 500 as one of the 500 largest US companies. Of course, a company's stock price is only one measure of value, and Netflix has done other things to achieve such growth. But the reality is that a multiplier mindset—when it comes to data—was at the core of their decision-making process. The same growth trend is true of Starbucks.

Before the company began using smart devices, big data, and AI, Starbucks was already successful, but not exponentially so. With new stores opening around the world, they were already a leader in what is fundamentally a commodity market—selling caffeinated beverages and related items to consumers. But by using data to know their customers better than they know themselves, Starbucks also propelled itself to become one of the country's 500 largest companies.

Reed Hastings believed that personalized entertainment was what people would want. He then went to the data to understand *precisely* what his customers really wanted, and then gave it to them. Starbucks also followed this path, basing their strategic business decisions on actual *data* collected from millions of customers' smart devices and analyzed using AI.

You do not need the massive resources of Netflix or Starbucks in order to utilize the true power of AI and big data. But the only way you will be able to take that leap is by learning everything you can about your customers—capturing as much of their data as possible and becoming obsessed with customer service.

Start by Asking the Right Questions

A few years ago, Uber started looking at the data collected from millions of customer rides all over the country. It found that many customers asked their drivers to stop at places like Starbucks along the route to their destination. They correlated rider and route data in key cities with locations of food and drink establishments and decided they could launch a new business that would use Uber drivers to deliver food to customers instead of making extra stops. And so, Uber Eats was born.

Those end-point innovations don't happen by accident. They happen because businesses rely on data to better understand their customers and develop ways to deliver the convenience and personalization that everyone expects now. Everything is about speed, ease, and personalization, like Amazon's one-click ordering. Customers love personalization and convenience, and because they are often deliverable using AI (think about Amazon's "Books You May Like" feature), they're also inexpensive. Looking at data reveals hidden weaknesses and opportunities. Leveraging data multiplies value.

But how do you know where to start looking? How do you find the right data? I suggest that my clients follow a three-step process:

Step One: Understand the problem you want to solve. Questions come before data. What do you want to know? Are you a delivery company looking for faster land routes to your customers? Are you a restaurant chain trying to discover why customers trying to order takeout online are getting frustrated and leaving your website? Or do you want to predict what they will order based on past choices? Which product should you launch, and which will be a big hit? What data are you looking for and why? Are you looking at the data so you can see what happened in the past, or are you looking at why it happened? Are you getting the data that will tell you what steps you should be taking?

Step Two: Align your data with your strategy. Your goal is to increase year-over-year profit by 20 percent. To achieve that, you need to use your data to exceed customer service expectations, inspire loyalty and referrals, and retain more customers. In turn, you need to create new internal business processes using data to maximize your operational efficiency and speed while also rolling out new products and services your customers will love. Additionally, you will need to recruit new employees and train your current workforce. Determine the actions you'll need to take to reach your goals, so you can figure out the kind of data you'll need and how to put it to work.

Step Three: Get actionable data. Collect the right data. You'll need historical data, such as financial transactions, customer surveys, and call center data. These reveal how your company performed and what your customers did in the past. But you'll also want predictive data, which suggests what your customers are likely to do in the future based on observed patterns. Study the data for insight; then you can apply machine learning or AI techniques to create a multiplier effect.

For example, a restaurant chain trying to reduce the number of customers abandoning online takeout orders might discover a chokepoint where customers are asked to provide their payment information and could adjust their process accordingly. You could also use sentiment analysis of call center recordings to address customer churn, as analyst Tosin Adekanye elegantly explained in 2021.[22] The possibilities are endless.

Netflix and Starbucks asked the right questions and pursued answers they knew would lead to innovation, and they had a bold outcome in mind for that innovation: becoming a platform for original content creation. They changed the game. In contrast, Blockbuster played catch-up after Netflix shook them out of complacency, but their culture and leadership meant they lacked the ability to truly innovate. With few exceptions,* other coffee chains and retailers have tried to mimic Starbuck's business decisions—but without basing their choices on actual data science.

The difference lies less with people's character or ability and more with their willingness to ask challenging questions and use the data to generate insights that will help them create the change their business needs.

---

* One such exception, Coda Coffee, is discussed in chapter 4.

CHAPTER 2

Understanding AI and Its Impact

In the 2013 film *Her*, a lonely Theodore Twombly (played by Joaquin Phoenix) installs an artificially intelligent virtual assistant that calls herself Samantha. Voiced by Scarlett Johansson, the AI companion proves not only capable of entirely reorganizing Theodore's life but turns out to be so charmingly engaging and human-like that Theodore falls in love with "her."

Toward the end of the movie, it's revealed that the fictional AI is processing millions of requests and having millions of simultaneous conversations behind the movie script. (In fact, this is what real AIs can do.) As a result, in the movie, "she" has the processing power to mine that big data set in order to simulate a personalized, albeit nonhuman, one-on-one relationship. But sadly, when Theodore finds out that Samantha is having those simultaneous conversations with millions of other people, he feels personally betrayed.

A darker Hollywood version of AI can be found in the *Terminator* franchise. In it, a network of powerful defense computers, SkyNet, gains self-awareness and decides humans are a threat to its existence. In the not-too-distant future, the storyline goes, it launches a preemptive nuclear war to wipe out most of humanity. It then designs and builds fearsome cyborgs—the eponymous "terminators"—to mop up the remaining humans and kill resistance fighters. Somehow, thanks to Arnold Schwarzenegger and Linda Hamilton, the AIs are defeated.

Both of these narratives about artificial intelligence are compelling stories, but they also feed our misconceptions. The point is not to personify the technology but to understand its potential benefits. The non-Hollywood reality is both more prosaic and, for businesses, more exciting.

The important fact is that AI is capable of extraordinary feats. It can free humans from repetitive tasks and exponentially increase the value that businesses can deliver. It can also identify useful patterns in gargantuan arrays of information, and generate surprisingly high-quality, original written, visual, and auditory content. At its most basic level:

> **AI encompasses any computing function**
> **that mimics the fundamental functions**
> **of human intelligence.**

AI analyzes incoming historical data to find repeating behaviors and outcomes, inferring patterns from that information, and learning from the patterns in order to better predict what will happen and recommend solutions. Basically, AI is trying to be as smart and intuitive as humans while potentially transcending human limitations like fatigue, boredom, the need to eat and drink, and bias.[*]

---

[*] As we will discuss in chapter 4, bias is not as easy to transcend as are our other limitations.

The Evolution of Artificial Intelligence

In the 1950s and '60s, the concept of AI was already in place, but we lacked the big data—and the computing power—to make it a reality. Companies were still working with large mainframe computers. Storage capacity was miniscule and processing speeds were slow. To illustrate, a typical iPhone today has over one million times more memory—and over 100,000 times the processing power—of the Apollo Guidance Computer used to land men on the moon in 1969.[1]

However, as Moore's Law* predicted, all that has changed. With time, the machines became smaller and their capacity to store and analyze data became far greater. They could perform billions of calculations per second. Finally, there was sufficient computing power to handle the influx of data for AI to handle.

Then along came the internet. Gradually, we all went online—communicating, sharing, creating. The world became smaller because people were now sharing their thoughts, preferences, and beliefs with each other and a growing number of companies and organizations. Suddenly, the world was flooded with data about people, businesses, and institutions. It became easier to start looking at trends, to find the patterns in what people were thinking, liked, and didn't like.

The nature of the data itself also changed. Early on, much of the world's data was *structured data*, which I alluded to in chapter 1. Structured data fits into predetermined formats—in rows and columns or records and fields. It is organized in a predictable way, such as banking records, name and address information from an online form, and ISBN information for books. It's the kind of data you might find in an Excel spreadsheet—typically heavy on dates, numbers, and organized or classified facts.

---

* In essence, Gordon Moore's 1970s maxim—still accepted today—holds that computer processing speeds or power will double every two years (www.mooreslaw.org).

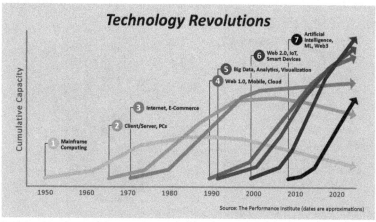

Successive waves of technology innovation have radically transformed the human experience. (We will discuss some of these developments, particularly Web 1–3, in chapter 9.)

However, as social media posts, emails, video, photographs, audio files, and other types of richer content became a larger part of the online world, the amount of *unstructured data* became overwhelming. Remember when I talked about depositing a check using a mobile app as an example of AI? The image of your check, which the AI software analyzes to determine if it's valid for deposit, is one kind of unstructured data. As you might expect, analyzing such data, which is rarely "labeled" and is often subtle or ambiguous in meaning, required unprecedented levels of computing sophistication. That was the essence of AI, and of its more sophisticated subsets.

Machine learning refers to artificial intelligence in which algorithms learn automatically and improve as they are exposed to more and more data. This can involve different degrees of supervision, using training data sets with varying levels of human oversight. For example, say that you want your AI system to be able to differentiate an image of a cat from that of a dog. You would

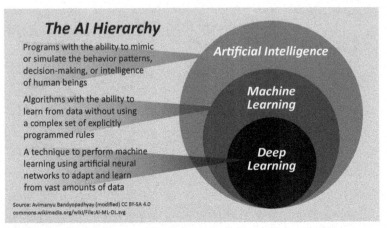

The AI Hierarchy

Programs with the ability to mimic or simulate the behavior patterns, decision-making, or intelligence of human beings

Algorithms with the ability to learn from data without using a complex set of explicitly programmed rules

A technique to perform machine learning using artificial neural networks to adapt and learn from vast amounts of data

Artificial Intelligence

Machine Learning

Deep Learning

Source: Avimanyu Bandyopadhyay (modified) CC BY-SA 4.0
commons.wikimedia.org/wiki/File:AI-ML-DL.svg

Artificial intelligence is an umbrella term that also includes machine learning and deep learning.

instruct the computer to analyze thousands or perhaps millions of images of all kinds of cats and dogs, each one labeled as such. Over time, the AI would "learn" which characteristics were associated with the idea of "cat" as opposed to "dog" or "human." Like a child who learns from repeated experiences, the machine learns with repeated exposure to data without being programmed.

Another example of machine learning is speech recognition. When you turn on a new iPhone, you can't use Siri until you follow the operating system's prompts to speak a predetermined set of voice commands, allowing the remote AI linked to your phone by the cloud (more on that in a little while) to learn to recognize your voice. In less than a minute, with a simple "Hey Siri," you can set reminders, launch apps, and call friends.

Finally, there is *deep learning*. This involves what computer scientists call *neural networks*—mathematical systems modeled on the neural structure of the human brain. The precise definition of this is complex, but the shorthand is that deep learning/neural networks employ multiple layers of processing and analysis simultaneously, allowing the system to identify far more complex characteristics and patterns within data than could be accomplished by simpler machine learning algorithms. In this way, deep learning mimics the dynamic activity of the human brain, which is highly plastic and adaptable. This requires enormous amounts of data and processing power, made possible by advances in cloud computing.

A well-known example of deep learning is Facebook's ability to identify individuals based on the facial features in photographs. (In November 2021, Facebook announced plans to shut down this system,[2] for reasons we will discuss in chapter 4.) This task is far more complex than learning to differentiate "cat" versus "dog" by recognizing that cats are more likely to have pointed ears and facial stripe patterns. Identifying a known individual by a photograph requires identifying thousands of visual data points and then correlating them with what could be hundreds, or thousands of text files associated with different user accounts that pair the person's name with images containing similar data points—all while accounting for variations in lighting, angle, image quality and other variables. Apple's Photos application uses deep learning in a similar way when it automatically groups user photos into "albums" based on date and location stamps and contextual clues such as facial features and physical surroundings.

This is what Google and OpenAI did with GPT-3, a natural language processing (NLP) AI. By "feeding" its neural net trillions of bits of textual data, they developed an artificial intelligence that learned the common sequences and cadences of human writing and speech. After all, human communication is fairly predictable. For example, if a friend accidentally texts you the partial phrase, "Would you like to go to the..." there are only so many words that make sense to complete that sentence—words like "movies," "store," or "ballgame." You can predict with high accuracy that when your friend texts the final word in her message, it won't be "bagel" or "infection." A neural net learns to make the same predictions. That's why after months of looking for patterns in titanic quantities of written material, GPT-3 was able to complete people's written sentences to a high degree of accuracy after they had typed only a few words. Humans, it turns out, are pretty predictable if you have enough data.

To date, GPT-3 has analyzed trillions of words in sources ranging from ebooks to blogs to social media and Wikipedia listings. As a result of this large-scale machine learning, it has developed an uncanny ability not just to compose startlingly compelling prose in microseconds but to write poetry, tweet, answer trivia questions, and even generate its own computer code.

The *New York Times* described one example[3] when one of the project's programmers asked GPT-3 to emulate pop psychologist Scott Barry Kaufman's writing voice. When asked the question, "How do we become more creative?" the AI's partial response was:

> **"I think creative expression is a natural byproduct of growing up in a diverse world. The more diverse the world is, the more you get exposed to different people, to different opportunities, to different places and to different challenges. And the more diverse that is, the more likely you'll be to be able to put the dots together to form something new."**

Reached for comment, the real Kaufman admitted that the AI-generated answer was a fairly accurate simulacrum of his real writing. But what makes GPT-3 so exciting is that it has been showing *emergent qualities*—abilities that its developers didn't expect it to have. The developers designed the AI to predict the next word in a sequence of words, and in taking in more than 175 billion language usage patterns over subsequent months, the system independently developed the ability to perform tasks it had not been designed to do, such as writing code. You could say that it evolved and continues to evolve.

AI customer service chatbots, or digital assistants that summarize emails for busy executives, are just the tip of the iceberg. As NLP systems like GPT-3 become more sophisticated, imagine a "bot" that could automatically write and update university textbooks with the latest research, or produce fine-tuned marketing copy based on an advertising agency's most recent batch of customer satisfaction data. Even more profound, AI language systems could assist a psychologist practicing telemedicine by composing exactly the right message to a patient who's having suicidal thoughts or correct a dangerous error in the computer code governing an autonomous vehicle while the vehicle is on the highway.

•———•

As you can imagine, fears and misunderstandings persist about what these technologies are, despite the fact that they are in use in virtually every segment of the economy. Think about it. If you order a recommended product from Amazon or use a mobile banking app to photograph a check to deposit it in your account, you're using AI. When your Nest thermostat automatically adjusts the temperature of your home in anticipation of your arrival from work, you're using a smart device. When your Fitbit tracks your daily steps and reminds you that to reach your average of the last six months, you need to walk another 2.2 miles today, that's big data at work. And when you access a file on Dropbox or share a Google Doc, you're using the cloud.

If you aspire to take your business to new levels of growth and profitability, it's time to move past the fears and misconceptions about technologies like AI and understand their extraordinary potential. I refer to AI, and its attendant technologies, including big data, smart devices, and cloud computing, as *multipliers*. They have the power to take the data that every company generates in the course of everyday operations, identify patterns that reveal critical weaknesses and opportunities, and supercharge that data to enable businesses to breed fierce customer loyalty, dominate existing markets, and innovate to create new markets. Deployed with precise strategy, these technologies can help your business grow revenues, profits, market share, and influence at a pace many times that of your competitors. Those that do not leverage them out of ignorance, comfort with the *status quo*, or fear of change will fall behind.

In other words, with these technologies, the extraordinary has become the ordinary. The missing piece lies in understanding how you, as one of the leaders of your business, can use them to reveal areas of untapped value hidden in your business model, acquire the relevant data to begin leveraging that value, and take the right actions at the right time to turn that value into black ink on your bottom line. Throughout this book, we will go deep into the thinking and strategies needed to precisely do that, but first, let's take a closer look at what these technologies *are*, how they work, and just as importantly, what they are *not*.

The Four Types of Analytics

Although the field of data analytics is almost as old as the web, it has changed dramatically over the past decade. In fact, the terms AI and analytics are sometimes used interchangeably, which is a mistake. While data analytics can be greatly enhanced by AI and machine learning, it can also be employed without their use.

Let's start by describing the four basic types of analytics:

Descriptive analytics is the most basic: reviewing a mass of data to determine what happened historically and whether that history occurred one hundred years ago or five minutes ago. **Diagnostic analytics** looks at repeating data points to determine the causal factors behind what happened, figuring out why it happened. Because they look at past events, these levels

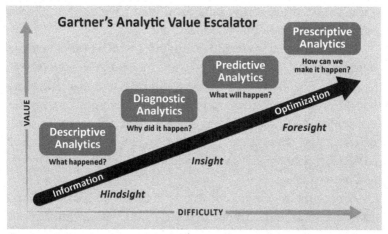

As analytical data become more forward facing (and more difficult to quantify), they increase in business value.

are considered hindsight. In business parlance, descriptive and diagnostic analytics are used to examine *lagging* indicators, as opposed to *leading* performance indicators.[4] These can benefit from the use of big data and AI, of course, but they do not require them.

With the third level, **predictive analytics**, we're getting into the heart of today's "personalization economy." Predictive analytics reviews patterns of past activity in order to predict what an individual, a group, or a complex system will do in the future. This approach is not perfect because it's based on probability, not certainty. In the introduction, I recounted the example of the 2002 Oakland Athletics, where they successfully used a pre-AI predictive data model—sabermetrics—to hire lower-salaried players based on nontraditional performance measurements. Their reasoning was that while the data's predictions might not pan out in any single game, the team's statistical advantage would win out over the entire season. (If a viable AI system had existed in the early 2000s, the Oakland data team may have done better, but even so, their model was successful enough.)

Finally, there is **prescriptive analytics**, which uses data to recommend solutions and draw conclusions that go beyond merely predicting results. This is where big data, AI, and machine learning are most often intertwined with the analytics process. For example, when an AI has enough unstructured data to identify patterns, and when it can be taught to assign meaning to those patterns, then it can develop the capacity to mimic human insight and reasoning.

A prominent example of this is the case of IBM Watson, a question-answering system first developed in the mid-2000s. More recently, using a Watson-based "Oncology Expert Advisor" tool, the project used a combination of machine learning and cancer research to make recommendations to clinicians.[5]

A more familiar example of this is any recommendation engine, such as that of Netflix or Amazon. When you're shopping on Amazon, after predictive analytics looks at your behavior patterns to determine what products you're likely to be interested in, prescriptive analytics selects the specific products to recommend to you based on the Amazon page you're on. It is also widely used in the healthcare industry, as we will explore in chapter 3.

While the technical specifics may be complex, the extraordinary implications of AI's power are clear. It can analyze enormous quantities of data, spot intricate patterns within billions of individual operations and data points, and recommend choices and products that not only meet customer needs but *anticipate* them. In an age when personalization has become the key to success in any business, AI offers the power to personalize products and services for millions of customers automatically, in real time, and with exceptional accuracy.

What AI Can Do

With trillions of bytes of data to learn from, ever-increasing processing speed and storage capacity, and the cloud providing high-speed internet connectivity from virtually anywhere, AI can already achieve an astonishing array of tasks. Here are some prominent examples:

- Google Duplex can manage appointments and make conversation with customers on the phone in realistic language.

- Major news organizations like the *Washington Post* and Reuters use AI to write basic news stories and real-time news updates, and sometimes, more complex and creative pieces, freeing human journalists to focus on more in-depth reporting.[6]

- Researchers at Loughborough University in England are developing a system based on deep learning that will detect and diagnose illnesses by "smelling" human breath.[7]

Other real-world AI examples include companies like Affectiva, developed in MIT's Media Lab in 2009, and Realeyes, a company that came out of Oxford University in 2007.[8] They are developing "artificial emotion intelligence" (also known as "affective computing"), which uses sensors, cameras, and deep learning to interpret human emotional responses to everything from movies to educational programs. Some remote learning systems already use eye movement tracking and AI to assess students' engagement with a lesson. If it detects that a student appears frustrated or discouraged, the AI can modify the lesson in real time to make it easier; if the student appears bored, the system can instantly make the lesson more challenging.

Then there is the array of visual, auditory, and motion processing needed to allow autonomous vehicles to operate safely.

AI systems can actually "see" the world around them based on a massive, ever-growing catalog of objects and people. Because real-world driving demands the ability to adapt instantly and respond in real time to a near-infinite number of unpredictable variables—such as traffic, pedestrians, obstacles, weather, emergencies, and breakdowns—the AI that controls autonomous vehicles is not yet ready for prime time, but it is not far away. In December 2020, General Motors subsidiary Cruise began testing autonomous vehicles on the streets of San Francisco's busy, dense Sunset District, with the ultimate aim of decreasing motor vehicle deaths.[9] It is safe to predict that within ten years, a majority of the passenger traffic in major cities like New York, Tokyo, and Berlin could be controlled by AI, not to mention much of the cargo traffic crisscrossing the country.

In other words, there is a great deal that AI can do when given sufficient data to learn about the customers, products, and services under a company's umbrella. If you run a home delivery company in a busy city, imagine AI computing optimal routes for your drivers to reach their destinations during rush hour, saving you time and fuel. If your company is engaging in a major campaign to reach new customers and increase market share, imagine an AI composing beautifully worded weekly e-newsletters to fresh leads and responding personally and uniquely to each reply or query. If you're in manufacturing, imagine a sensor-powered AI monitoring your equipment 24/7, predicting potential failures before they happen, diagnosing needed repairs, and automatically dispatching human engineers by text message to fix the problem—without interrupting your factory's operations.

AI can automate repetitive tasks, identify actionable patterns in data, coordinate robotic process automation (RPA), and communicate instantly with millions of people. The potential is almost limitless.

Big Data

Big data is the fuel that powers artificial intelligence. Without enormous amounts of data to analyze and learn from, AI would consist of massive processing power with nothing to process. The two go hand in hand.

As I described earlier, structured data are predictable and binary, the kind of data that systems commonly accumulate using forms and fields. Structured data largely consist of the kind of data points we think of as the contents of a database: names, email addresses, phone numbers, demographic information like age and gender, tax records, purchasing histories, and medical records. When the information age started in the 1960s and 1970s, huge companies like Oracle and IBM were all working with structured data. The world knew how to put the data in a structured format like you would use to put your data in an Excel sheet.

Unstructured data challenged that infrastructure. It didn't just mean an exponential increase in new data, but a new *type* of data. Beginning in the 1990s, unstructured data exploded with the invention of the world wide web, first through "walled garden" services like America Online, and later when the web became ubiquitous thanks to consumer browsers like Netscape Navigator and Internet Explorer. Long before social media existed, the demands of processing unstructured data—such as images, video, and emails—began to overwhelm the computing capacity of big corporations and forced them to evolve new tools for processing and analyzing this torrent of new data. This is when the concept of big data came into its own.

Even with faster systems, companies had to transition from regular databases that stored structured data in organized data warehouses to "data lakes," vast pools of raw data dumped in unorganized formats. They had the challenge of finding a way to take all this raw unstructured data and use it. Those leaders who understood the potential and started making sense of unstructured data early included Amazon, Netflix, and Apple. They took the lead because they understood that big data meant having a deep understanding of what customers wanted, needed, and cared about, and such knowledge was the key to the future.

Big data has three basic facets:

- **Data collection at scale.** Companies and organizations collect data about their customers using every means possible to discover their preferences and activities, from cookies to online forms and surveys.

- **Data processing/mining.** Big data companies extract information from huge complex data sets, often using algorithms or machine learning to read billions of data fields, draw inferences, and identify patterns.

- **Analyzing and acting on data.** Companies like Netflix determine the utility of their data, using them to do things like develop and refine new products, personalize product offerings, improve customer service, and/or increase the precision of marketing campaigns. Political campaigns use big data to micro-target messaging to specific voter demographics—for example, Cuban Americans or family farmers—based on those groups' historical voting patterns and areas of concern.

Another way to view big data is by using the "three v's" model.[10] Its sheer *volume* is only one factor. Equally important are its complex *variety*, from structured easily classifiable information to unstructured seemingly random bits, and its ever-increasing speed and direction—or *velocity*—at which it can be processed.

Of course, there are other "v" factors to consider, including veracity and value, which we explore throughout this book.

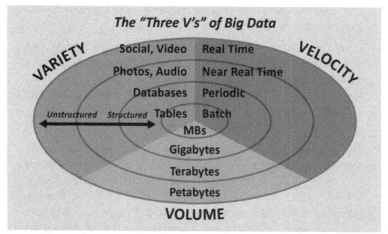

The growth of big data is characterized not only by its volume, but also by its complexity and the speed with which it can be processed, via artificial intelligence.

The Potential of Big Data

Big data is most important for giving companies and organizations clarity about themselves, their customers or members, and the way forward. If you don't have a clear idea of where you're going, it's hard to build technology or a company. Big data gives you clear vision of inefficiencies in your business model, underserved corners of your market, products, or services your customers are asking for, and areas where cost savings are possible. Once you have that big-picture data, you can break it down into smaller pieces to execute on it to derive profits or organizational improvement.

> Let's suppose I am launching a new line of blue jeans in Boston, and my goal is to get a 20 percent revenue increase in that market over my previous products. I need to understand if my product will actually give me that increase. Most importantly, I need to understand the buying behavior of my target audience.

This must be done with specific intent. What is true for one city may not work for another.

I know from past data collection that the consumer most likely to buy the product I'm selling is a college graduate under age twenty-five. That's a great start. Now, I can use my database to home in on the specific buying patterns and product preferences of those people using resources like historical purchasing data and product and customer satisfaction surveys.

My data tell me that my optimal customers are artistic people living in Cambridge and Charlestown between twenty-three and twenty-eight years old, and that they are very interested in colored jeans—yellow, red, pink, green, and so on. Now I have a specific market segment for testing, so then I connect with that audience using AI. I'll have my system launch a digital marketing campaign using text messages with AI responses, AI-designed graphics shared on social media, AI-produced music clips, and perhaps environmental advertising using AI-generated messaging based on my data—all messages constantly being A/B tested by AI. (This involves two alternative message sets, with the results of each set tracked.)

Now I'm building a brand and starting to generate inbound sales traffic. I assess the effectiveness of everything, adapt, and keep moving. The biggest use cases in this scenario involve customer satisfaction and behavior, although such data can also be used for employee satisfaction, process improvement, and even inventory control.

Big data helps you achieve clarity. Then you can set your goals—innovation, efficiency, a new brand, a new business model, or whatever else will achieve a multiplier effect. Then you can progress to activity, which could be refining operations, launching new products, or a hundred other options. With the right data, you can feed it into an algorithm that will predict how more efficient operations will reduce your costs on an annualized basis or how many units you're likely to move during the first quarter after your product launch.

With big data guided by artificial intelligence and machine learning, business decisions need not be guided by gut instinct, bias, and emotion. And, with the support of increasingly afford- able devices and the cloud, big data can be utilized by nearly everyone.

Robotics and Smart Devices

To put it simply, a robot is a machine that learns by analyzing real-time data and turns that learning into activity in the physical world and, occasionally, the nonphysical world. Like AI, robots are the subject of fear and misunderstanding fueled by popular fiction. But the reality is less dramatic and more promising for businesses and organizations.

Robotics has been around since the 1950s, but the field did not take off at the time because the of the missing components of big data and artificial intelligence. Today, big data-powered AI helps machines do useful things—without human intervention. Robotic systems have now become more responsive and more like human behavior because now they have enough data on humans plus the ability to process the data quickly and learn from it.

As a result, we now have autonomous cars and Tesla man- ufacturing plants run entirely by robots. We have entire "smart buildings" in which the security and environmental systems mon- itor themselves and adjust automatically. We have smart watches, smart televisions, smart appliances, and smart thermostats—all part of something known as *the internet of things*, or IoT.

We also have literal anthropomorphic robots like Sophie, which can hold realistic conversations, or Embodied's Moxie, which helps improve the social and emotional skills of elementary school–aged children,[11] or the Tombot Jennie, a hyper-realistic emotional support robot puppy for seniors that behaves like a real dog.[12] Despite our apprehensions and the fact that robots have not attained widespread popularity, their benefits are undeniable.

Robotic applications have demonstrated their benefits in health-care, transportation, home appliances, and elsewhere, and are likely to continue doing so—*without* causing an apocalypse.

Of course, the field is not limited to devices with a mechanical or motorized aspect. Smartphones, tablets, and wearable devices—even ordinary PCs—each have a "robotic" component. That is, they all use big data and AI to collect data on human behavior and, in many cases, process the results to meet the needs of the humans who use them. For example, a mobile device's GPS-aware wireless signal and its built-in accelerometer supply a constant stream of data that, when processed using AI, simplifies and/or directs our activity. One example is the health app, pre-installed on many smartphones, which can measure steps taken in a day and even record vital statistics to analyze health-related trends over time. Such devices also constantly record our purchasing decisions and other activities, creating a massive store of data that can be utilized to benefit those who understand its value. Even internet-connected home appliances, security systems, and temperature control systems collect and utilize vast amounts of data to support human decisions and/or make them autonomously.

In every meaningful sense, our personal smart devices are robots. You could even consider Amazon's fully autonomous Go retail stores to be "robot environments." Customers download the Amazon Go app, present a QR code for scanning as they walk into the store, grab what they want off the shelves, and walk out as the store's automated system debits their accounts. No humans required.

The Implications Are Clear

We are bringing robotics and smart devices together with AI and the power of big data to address hundreds of thousands of disparate human and business needs. The biggest use cases have been in manufacturing and healthcare. Robots are assisting the aging population with everything from easing the pain or isolation and performing physical therapy to communicating and ensuring medication compliance. Robotic surgery assisted by AI is also quickly becoming a reality. In manufacturing, we have robotic process automation, in which thousands of mundane functions of a manufacturing or fabrication facility are controlled and monitored by AI, including robotic assembly and even robots repairing damaged or malfunctioning systems. Robots help improve processes, reduce errors, and even control a substantial amount of traffic in consumer financial services—the so-called "robo-advisor."

Robotics and smart devices are where real change can happen in business because this is where big data and AI can have an effect on the physical world. For example, companies begin to see cost savings and higher profits when they put their data to work designing improved control surfaces that make aircraft more fuel efficient. The same happens when they use sensor-rich drones that can handle delivery of smaller parcels instead of human drivers in gas-guzzling trucks. Similarly, efficiency increases when they employ AI systems that enable customer service chatbots to handle 90 percent of incoming support calls, allowing them to cut payroll or assign customer service reps to more complex issues that require human attention.

A powerful example of robot-assisted consumer protection occurred during the COVID-19 pandemic. Many small businesses found that their survival depended on being able to deliver packages, food, or supplies directly to people's homes. The trouble was package thieves figured this out as well, and so-called "porch pirate" theft incidents skyrocketed. However, some small companies came up with a solution using smart devices. Knowing that most new cars since 2017 have onboard apps that allow smart phones to activate basic functions, these businesses made their customers a proposal: when you place an order, we'll send you a text message asking for permission to unlock your personal vehicle using a single-use code.

If the customer agreed, after an order was placed, a company driver would approach the customer's car or SUV wherever it was parked, unlock it using this one-time-only code, place the customer's order in the cargo area, and close and relock the vehicle. The code would expire so it could never be used again, and the company would know the identity of the delivery person and the precise time they were at the vehicle. The customer would get their no-contact order securely. It was a brilliant solution to a global problem.

With improvements such as smaller, lighter robots and devices, better AI, smaller microprocessors, and ever-greater stores of data, we're entering a cyclical system where technology becomes ever more useful. Big data systems continue to capture and catalog quintillions of data points. Ever more sophisticated and powerful AI algorithms and neural nets analyze that data, learning to better identify areas of hidden value and predict human needs. Robots and smart devices respond to those needs with a speed and anticipation that seems prescient at times. By interacting with consumers, business-to-business customers, and the environment, smart devices collect still more data, and the cycle continues.

Advanced Machines Are Changing the Game

The biotech company Medtronic is one example of a business that has leveraged the versatility of robotics to achieve quantum leap growth. The impact of the COVID-19 pandemic has made distance medicine a must-have capability for many hospitals and surgical centers, and robot-assisted surgery (RAS) is at the core of that capability.

Medtronic's soft-tissue robotics system, Hugo,[13] has begun to encroach on the market share of leader incumbent Intuitive

Surgical, positioning Medtronic to not only show 37 percent sales growth in the fourth quarter of its current fiscal year, but to anticipate $100 million to $300 million in annual revenue from RAS by fiscal year 2023. The company also plans to spend more on R&D than at any time in its history. In other words, advanced AI-enabled robotics has taken Medtronic from a fringe player in remote medicine to a change agent.

It would be hard to find a better example of the power of AI and smart devices to take a brand from unknown to global player status than the former Nest Labs. Co-founded by former Apple engineers Tony Fadell and Matt Rogers, the company rolled out its flagship product in 2011: the Nest Learning Thermostat.[14] Programmable, connected to the cloud via Wi-Fi, sensor-equipped, and capable of learning user preferences from behavior patterns, the Nest became a sensation, spawning related products such as smart smoke detectors and security cameras, and establishing the idea of the "smart home" in the public consciousness. It was the direct progenitor of "smart speaker" devices like Amazon's Alexa.

But the proof of the transformative wealth-creating power of smart devices came in 2014, when Google bought the 150-employee Nest Labs for $3.2 billion. Today, the Nest brand lives on in Google Nest devices, including "mesh" home wi-fi systems and the Google Home smart speaker. Not bad for a four-year-old startup.

Cloudy with a Chance of Profit

Connecting that entire technological ecosystem—that virtuous cycle of learning, information, and efficiency—is the internet in the form of cloud computing. Cloud computing makes vast data processing power available remotely by using a vast array of internet-connected servers. So, instead of having to physically host their own AI (which would be impossible, given the size of the computers needed to process all the data), robots and real-time AI systems like Siri and Alexa can connect nearly instantaneously to remote servers and processors, which handle the heavy lifting of analyzing data and sending instructions to sensors, servos, and other physical systems.

The cloud is about making processing speed, computational power, data structure, and complicated analysis available to any organization without a huge investment in infrastructure. The best example of this is Amazon Web Services (AWS), which accounts for 32 percent of the public cloud market.[15] AWS, Microsoft, and other cloud providers serve online businesses by making their robust data "back end" easily available to companies anywhere in the world for an affordable price.

Mid-sized companies benefit from the cloud because they no longer need large data centers. The cloud is perfect for powering IoT devices—from farm irrigation sensors to home security systems to "smart toothbrushes"—because those devices often use Wi-Fi or even 5G wireless connectivity to send and receive relatively small amounts of data quickly. Where the cloud isn't performing well enough is in big data environments. The processing speed and data infrastructure simply isn't there—yet.

In the early 2000s, Apache Hadoop was developed as an open-source framework to make big data computation possible. It was originally on massive local computer clusters but was eventually replaced by cloud computing. The promise was that unstructured data would go into the cloud and be processed at a higher speed, but the infrastructure to handle all that unstructured data remotely is not quite there. The cloud's promise of connectivity and access to data anywhere is not completely fulfilled—yet. However, as Moore's Law continues to play out and with the development of quantum computing, processing speeds will continue their inexorable rise and storage capacity will continue to grow. Eventually, the cloud's utility will extend to operations at nearly any scale.

Think Like Tesla and Amazon

Elon Musk's Tesla has long been at the bleeding edge of utilizing the cloud's potential. It is no exaggeration to state that without its use of the cloud, Tesla would be just another electric car maker. For years, Tesla's driver profiles have been stored within its vehicles, allowing drivers to program all of their preferred configurations for seat position, music settings, mirrors, and other equipment. Each driver profile is either linked to a driver's smartphone via the Tesla App or the Tesla key itself, which allows the vehicle to sense the presence of the driver and reconfigure the car according to the desired settings. Now, that capacity is being transferred to the cloud via the Tesla Network.

This will not only enable the storage of more driver data and media, but it will also allow Tesla to use cloud-based algorithms to guide and "train" autonomous vehicles. Data for Tesla's AI system will also come from the ride-sharing service the company hopes to launch in 2022 to compete with Uber and Lyft.[16]

Amazon Web Services (AWS) is another great example. In the early 2000s, Amazon's IT team decided that the way to deal with fast-growing seasonal ecommerce traffic and other bottlenecks was to focus on a "fast, reliable, cheap" architecture. In 2006, AWS was opened to the public, allowing developers to access on-demand cloud computing—quickly and cheaply—as the back end for stores, media sites, gaming sites, and more.

Over the past fifteen years, Amazon's "ecommerce as a service" platform has evolved into EC2, a virtual machine service, Glacier, a low-cost cloud storage service, and the S3 storage system. Today, AWS accounts for about 63 percent of total operating income. That's not just cloud; it's a bolt of lightning.

Learn from Tesla and Amazon: migrate your business to the cloud. Forget hosting a big data environment in-house. Start collecting your data and using the remote power of cloud computing and AI to understand what your data are telling you—to innovate, create efficiencies, or use the latest technologies like IoT, robotics, and analytics to figure out the *implications* of your data for your business. Then you can apply that insight appropriately to your business use cases, instead of sitting back and waiting for change to happen—and ultimately falling behind.

Look at Netflix and Starbucks and the examples described in the next chapter. In the end, their rise isn't about technology. It's about more than business intelligence. It's about the impact of AI and related technology in applying the insights that the data give them and acting accordingly. It goes back to strategic thinking. When Netflix did what it did, streaming was primitive. Data processing speed was lower. Their algorithm wasn't as good. That didn't matter because they knew the questions to ask and the business problems they were trying to address.

The good news is that you can ask those questions too.

CHAPTER 3

What Do Pizza and Cosmetics Have in Common?

By now, you may be eager to jump ahead to the "how to" parts of the book, but I'll ask for your forbearance. The following examples will give you a broader context and some important new details that will make your implementation of data and AI solutions a more well-rounded experience.

The power of the AI Factor lies in its potential to reveal and maximize additional value in virtually any industry. That value is in the data, whether it's now in your possession or just a potential waiting to be collected and used. Think of data as an abundant renewable natural resource—one that cannot be exhausted but can certainly be wasted. By using artificial intelligence and its related technologies, anyone can harvest that resource and use it to multiply the value of their endeavors.

No matter what a company's products or services are—or whether it's designed for profit or not—every human endeavor generates data. For example, whenever you sell a widget, you've created all kinds of data. It can be *structured* data (what, how many, when, to whom, at what price). The data can also be *unstructured* (a picture, a tweet about it from the buyer, a pattern of purchase behavior, one of a thousand other seemingly random events stemming from that sale. Or it could be something unrelated to a physical product, like a charitable donation. The structured data are abundant, but so are the unstructured data related to that single event.

Every business or nonprofit activity is a constant source of its own data. Although that body of data is invariably connected to other entities and people, it is unique to that organization's business or purpose. Collectively, it may seem overwhelming. But in reality, it is an ocean of opportunity for those who know how to use it.

Two Approaches, Two Different Outcomes

In chapter 1, I introduced my own modified version of a common business positioning mechanism that I called the four quadrants.*
Based on a company's willingness to take risks and innovate, and/or its inherent growth potential, it can be described as an *optimizer*, a *contender*, an *extender*, or a *multiplier* business. As we will explore in part two, businesses in any of these four quadrants can utilize AI and big data to their advantage. In fact, a company can use their experience with AI in one quadrant to move their business model forward, ultimately becoming a multiplier business.

For example, by using big data and AI to lower costs and improve their process, an optimizer company may well discover new market potential and move to an extender strategy. Or they could use the experience to take more risks and develop new products, adopting a contender strategy. Ultimately, any company

---

* See page XX. <insert after paging>

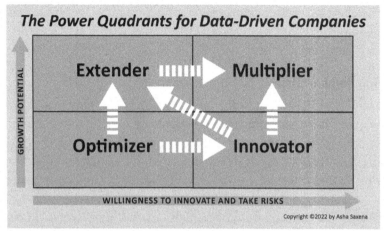

Any business or nonprofit can benefit from AI and big data now and leverage that experience to move forward.

can leverage their expertise with AI and, with the right mindset, progress along the path to becoming a multiplier business.

This chapter will explore companies that were willing to make the journey using AI to uncover and exploit the value of their data. Although the nature of their products and services differs widely, what they have in common is an appreciation for their data's potential and a willingness to use it in new ways. They did not start out as multiplier businesses but ultimately became so—daring to disrupt their own business models and literally follow the data. The outcome of this approach is both financial and reputational success.

The cautionary part of this chapter will be to note some companies who refused the journey. Even major brands with storied reputations and huge volumes of data have failed to thrive—or have even gone out of business—because they failed to see the value of their own data or were unwilling to use AI and its related technologies to their advantage.

The good news is that AI and big data are more accessible than ever. Although not without difficulty and risk, they are the keys to extraordinary success.

The Domino's Effect

Leading up to the 2008–2009 recession, the Domino's Pizza chain was suffering the effects of a depressing market trend. By the late 1990s, the 6,000-store franchise had become the leading US pizza delivery company, filing a successful IPO in 2004. However, during that time, delivery pizza was steadily losing market share to frozen pizza and rival fast-food chains. The recession-generated declines in consumer spending made things worse. Many of their competitors responded by cutting prices, but Domino's responded with a multiplier strategy utilizing smart devices and data to reinvent their approach to marketing.[1]

The Domino's brand image was not stellar in the mid-2000s. Focus groups and newly emerging online forums routinely criticized their product, including the pizza's infamous "cardboard crust." However, instead of hiding from the negative criticism, the company embraced the data and began looking for ways to exploit it.

As typified by the company's memorable "Oh Yes We Did" TV campaign,[2] the company turned the critical comments into a mandate to completely change every aspect of its pizza recipes, eventually using the experience to create a self-deprecating documentary-style ad.[3] The results were encouraging. Reinventing their pizza recipes—and highlighting their response to the negative data—was followed by a 32.2 percent increase in sales. The company's stock price also rose from around five to thirty dollars a share. But the company's creative use of data was only just beginning.

Logged-in Domino's customers can participate in either the Idea Forum or the Project Assignments portion of the "Think Oven" process. New ideas are discussed and voted upon. Projects undergo an ideation process, where proposed solutions are discussed, shared, and voted on. Both data sets are further developed into new Domino's business activity. (Diagram adapted from Domino's March 14, 2011 presentation, as published in *Medium*.[4])

In 2012, the company launched "Think Oven," a Facebook page that actively solicited customer ideas—including everything from new menu items and suggestions on sustainability to projects like new Domino's uniform designs.[5] (Cash prizes were awarded for the best ideas, which were hand-selected from over 10,000 submissions.) The site gained over one million new Facebook fans and—more importantly—a trove of valuable crowdsourced data. The company has been proactive in the use the data, and in the development of additional apps to better understand their customer's behavior and anticipate their needs.

As these measures gained traction, the company began to radically reinvent its business model, increasingly using data and digital technology to transform it from a fast-food franchise to, as company executives put it:

> ...an *"e-commerce company that* **happens to sell pizza."**[6]

These initiatives took on many forms, many of which continue today. They include an online tracker and voice ordering app, allowing customers to buy pizza using Slack, Facebook Messenger, Twitter, the Domino's mobile app, and with smart TVs using Alexa and Google Assistant. By 2018, over half of Domino's sales come from mobile devices, including a "one tap" feature that lets customers repeat an order without entering new information.

The data initiative that started with Think Oven has expanded, with continuous A/B testing and refinement of its predictive analytics. In addition to expanding its social media presence—gathering and using data via its loyalty program—Domino's has also deployed AI virtual assistants (nicknamed "DOM") to help customers with orders. It is also partnering with Ford's self-driving car program to develop future autonomous delivery systems.

The company's precipitous and sustained stock price increase, while not the only indicator of value, is impressive evidence of Domino's multiplier strategy. It is driven not only by its deliberate use of AI, big data, and smart devices, but also by its leaders' willingness to break old business models and pursue new ones.

The strategy is still working. In 2017, Domino's overtook Pizza Hut as the world's largest pizza chain.[7] It's compound annual growth rate (CAGR) is at 9 percent, and its stock performance is not only better than that of its restaurant competitors but it also outperforms many non-restaurant "highfliers" in the US market.[8]

Not bad for a company whose pizza crust was once compared to cardboard.

Because It's Worth It

L'Oréal is a 115-year-old firm that behaves like a Silicon Valley startup. The international beauty products company began when a French chemist developed a coloring formula and began selling it to hairdressers in Paris. Today, the company has *expanded* its focus on science—from the chemistry of their products to big data and artificial intelligence.

In 1997, The Harvard Business School published a study of L'Oréal's plan to revitalize the marketing for their Plénitude line of skincare products.[9] The goal was, among other things, to broaden the brand's appeal to a mass audience. Data on customers' perceptions was a key element of the research, measuring responses on the products' price and availability as well as its appeal to different age and social demographics.

One aspect of L'Oréal's customer research involved a process called perceptual mapping. By taking the brand attribute ratings of all survey respondents, and plotting the results in a two-dimensional manner, they were able to visualize the relationship of the Plénitude line with competing products. This enabled them to make meaningful changes in everything from packaging, store displays, and advertising to SKU consolidation, distribution strategy, and pricing. As a result of these efforts, the product line's perception in the market began to change, and its sales grew significantly.

Using data in the late 1990s helped the company make meaningful changes and increase profitability, but it did not end there. Since then, L'Oréal has become known as:

> *"arguably, the most digitally innovative*
> *beauty company in the world."*[10]

The challenge was a formidable one, given the complex nature of the company's many product lines and customer habits, as I learned from conversations with the company's Chief Information Officer for the Americas, Susannah Greenberg.

> "Consumer data is very valuable" Greenberg said. "We believe we can serve our consumers better when we understand them better. And so, over time, we built our own consumer data platform—in a privacy-safe way—including data they are willing to explicitly tell us as well as, in some cases, implied data. For example, if somebody clicks a lot on a particular category, we can imply that they're currently interested in that category. Generally speaking, we learn as much as we can about the people."
>
> The collected data have practical effects far beyond product recommendation. "We're always asking, 'What can the data tell us and what questions do I have that I would like the data to answer?'" Greenberg illustrated this complexity when it came to issues like replenishment rates—the fact that people often use twice as much shampoo as they do conditioner, which has implications throughout the life cycle of multiple products.

In 2012, the company started its US-based "Connected Beauty Incubator" division within its already-formidable research group. Assigned to focus on tech innovation and disruption, the group has applied big data, AI, smart devices, and the cloud in new ways, including:

- **Using big data and AI to guide product development.** Partnering with cloud integration company Talend, L'Oréal collects over fifty million pieces of data per day, using that enormous data lake to develop thousands of new product formulas every year.[11] The purpose of the group, according to their experimental data intelligence lead, Philippe Benivay, is to deliver services that have not even been considered yet. "In the globalized beauty industry," he said, "L'Oréal must innovate ever faster to meet the desires and needs of customers looking for new products and services that respect their bodies and the environment."

The process correlates the company's vast research data on customers' perceptions of product performance, in real time, with its physiochemical definition of formulas and raw materials—as well as other data on safety and toxicology. By using AI to parse the data, this results in conclusions that are used by scientists to imagine and develop new products. It also serves to inform other company departments and encourage their feedback.

The success of L'Oréal's data-driven, localized product development is remarkable, covering 130 countries across twenty-eight international brands. According to cloud partner IBM, that success across so many culturally diverse regions is due to the synchronized, high-quality nature of the data.[12]

- **Using AI and AR to drive business performance.**[13] In 2015, the company launched Makeup Genius, an augmented reality (AR) based mobile app that allows users to "see" the results of hair color and makeup choices on their smartphones. The user simply uses the device camera to upload an image of their face, selects different products, and uses the sliding "before and after" feature for the results. Of course, it also provides users an easy way to order the products they like. L'Oréal later acquired a more advanced skin diagnostic system, ModiFace, using live video to simulate product use. They have even developed a "smart hairbrush," which uses a conductivity sensor, an accelerometer, and other technology to send data to an AI-based algorithm, resulting in personalized product recommendations on hair care.

In addition to smart device-driven ecommerce, which accounts for a fast-growing portion of company revenues, the company uses AI to streamline the recruiting and hiring process. To process over a million yearly job applications (to fill about 15,000 openings), the company's chatbot, Mya, handles routine questions on things like availability and visa status. Then, an AI-enabled system, Seedlink, analyzes candidates' responses to open-ended questions. Besides saving hundreds of screening hours, the tool has identified candidates that were overlooked in the traditional resume review process.

- **Using smart devices and AI to reinvent "conversational marketing."** After careful study, L'Oréal also launched the first of several planned Facebook Messenger "bots," using AI to help consumers find the right beauty products and learn more about those consumers in the process. The company is still working on safeguards to make sure their brand does not appear next to extremist content. However, it is clearly using AI to shorten the time between a consumer's discovery of a product and the "moment of truth" when they actually buy it. "Digital [is all about] creating a connection with consumers," according to Chief Digital Officer Lubomira Rochet. "By getting the right insight and products…[it] has become the backbone of our marketing operations."[14]

All this innovation clearly puts L'Oréal in the multiplier category, as its remarkable business growth indicates. Systematically, and over the course of several years, the company leveraged its own customer data to improve—or totally reinvent—its business models. It used data and AI to create new, intrinsically desirable products, inspire deeper customer engagement and loyalty, and develop an ecommerce platform that is, to a data scientist, truly beautiful.

AI and Smaller Companies

Up to this point, the examples of multiplier strategies have involved large, mainly international companies—although they certainly didn't start out that way. A reason for this is that publicly traded companies offer a convenient, admittedly simplified way to measure growth acceleration—namely, their stock price. This is inspiring, but for smaller, mostly private companies, the benefits are a bit harder to quantify. Nevertheless, the benefits of AI and its related technologies are real and can apply to companies of almost any size.

For smaller companies, it's important to note that implementing artificial intelligence and big data is not something one does all at once. As we will see in part two, the best strategy is to select *one* key area—never more than two or three—in which to apply the principles of AI.

More Effective Hiring

For companies of any size, the grueling process of recruiting and hiring new talent is one such area. The number of unfilled job openings, a problem amplified by the pandemic, is a staggering burden to businesses and an impediment to company growth. Unfortunately, the traditional HR screening process is time-consuming, costly, and often fails to find and engage the right talent. Add to that the burden of hiring internationally and finding talent from different countries and cultures.

The good news is that all the resumes, emails, voicemails, and text messages entering the HR orbit are *unstructured data*. That means they are fertile ground for AI.

AI developer RChilli has developed a data-centric approach to this problem, one that has been incorporated by staffing companies, recruiters, as well as mid- to large-sized companies with perennial hiring difficulties. Typically integrated with job boards and applicant tracking software (ATS), the RChilli system incorporates a multilingual parser for resumes submitted in Word and other formats. Routine information, such as contact numbers and email addresses, is extracted with relative ease, but very often a resume contains important information in the unstructured text. So, RChilli's AI component uses NLP to extract that data and automatically convert it into relevant information.

The system can do the same for social media feeds and other unstructured data sources. It also recently introduced new privacy safeguards, including compliance with the European Union's General Data Protection Regulation (GDPR), and it can even filter for unconscious bias. The resulting big data set can then be processed, using a skills and jobs taxonomy, to identify promising candidates for specific positions and job requirements.

The use of this level of AI has not gone unnoticed. Human resources consulting and technology firm Berkshire Associates successfully incorporated RChilli into its widely used ATS, BalanceTRAK.[15] From its origins in automating affirmative action plans, Berkshire's AI-enabled system now has significantly enhanced the job candidate's experience and improved recruiters' productivity.

Midsized cloud developer Phenom People also benefited from this approach. The company found that the recruitment modules of PeopleSoft, Oracle Cloud, and SAP could be far more efficient in growing its skilled workforce of 9,000-plus employees. By integrating the RChilli AI parser into these systems, the company was able to reduce the cost per hire by 60 percent, making the entire talent acquisition process easier. They also found it reduced the employee attrition rate, since their HR department was better able to match with jobs and skills that hires would find most satisfying.

This approach has also been adopted by larger companies, including the global payroll processing powerhouse ADP.[16] The RChilli parser greatly reduced the company's need to manually enter data and shortlist candidates from large numbers of submitted resumes. It even processed candidate data from emails and social media, reducing the cost of hiring by 58 percent.

Data-Based Marketing

Another common application of AI—one that smaller companies could adopt with relative ease—is in the area of digital marketing. With the explosion of media channels over the past two decades, companies often struggle with the sheer volume of data—mostly unstructured—that can erupt from the web, social media, and mobile apps. Search optimization and paid search advertising sound promising at first, but smaller marketing departments are soon overwhelmed with too much data and little time to sort it out.

Digital agency NoGood has added an AI twist to its array of marketing services, including SEO, paid search, social ads, and funnel conversion rate marketing. Common to all these is their approach to unstructured data, utilizing artificial intelligence to make sense of flood of user activity, distilling it into meaningful actions for content marketing campaigns.

Extracting meaningful information from such data has obvious benefits. NoGood's approach resulted in a 350 percent increase in new client revenue and a 50 percent increase in existing client revenue for Fratelli Carli, an online seller of Italian food products.[17] The application of AI allowed the company to analyze the interests, preferences, and psychographics of their customers, rapidly test new personas, and design personalized retention efforts over multiple media channels.

The same data approach was applied for Steer, a subscription-based electric car service that provides alternative to buying or leasing vehicles.[18] Using AI-enabled product prototyping, competitive research, and funnel end user experience analytics, NoGood was able to provide effective media management for the company's far-reaching advertising and marketing campaigns. The results were a 600 percent increase in web traffic, a 320 percent increase in conversion rates, and a 37 percent increase in month-over-month revenue.

Healthier Choices

The healthcare industry is enormous. It includes very large pharma companies, device manufacturers, insurance companies, and healthcare providers. However, it also includes many smaller companies, hospitals, and clinics—many of which struggle to cope with mountains of data.

The opportunities for using big data and AI in the healthcare realm are enormous. A 2020 medical journal article[19] identified some significant benefits, including, among other observations, the following improvements:

- *Faster and more accurate diagnostics* obtained by loading the results of a physical exam to a system capable of considering all possibilities and automatically identifying deficiencies, illnesses, and even available treatments.
- *Reduction of errors* caused by human fatigue.
- *AI-based surgical assistance* allowing human surgeons to perform minimally invasive procedures more accurately.
- *Improved radiology results* providing more comprehensive interpretations of images from MRIs, fetal imaging, and other unstructured data.

Many of these improvements will improve quality of care, lower costs, or both. These include virtual assistants for Alzheimer's patients and early detection of melanomas using infrared light to algorithmically evaluate pigmented lesions.[20] It also includes benefits such as dramatic reductions in hospital admissions. In 2020, *Forbes* reported[21] on a study by Clare Medical of New Jersey where an AI-based diagnostic tool accurately forecast a variety of serious clinical outcomes. Of those patients, most of whom were elderly or otherwise at risk, over 50 percent did not require hospitalization after the forecast was made known, giving them time to take preventive measures. According to a Clare Medical summary, a single hospital admission of an elderly patient with multiple comorbidities can cost more than $30,000 and put the patient at further risk.[22] So, the introduction of AI clearly has both an economic and a social value multiplier effect.

Finally, another hospital has demonstrated the potential for AI to both improve quality of healthcare and reduce its costs. In 2020, Hackensack Medical Center became the first hospital in New Jersey to implement an AI-powered surgical training program.[23] The C-SATS system enables the hospital's surgical robotics team to track performance securely, enhance their skills continuously, and improve overall patient outcomes.

A Missed Opportunity

No discussion of successful multiplier strategies would be complete without a cautionary tale. There are too many companies who simply refuse to make the journey into AI and big data—even with an entry-level optimizer strategy. One such example is the Eastman Kodak Company.

Beginning in the 1880s, the Kodak camera was one of the most innovative, and profitable technologies ever developed for a mass audience. It was an extremely simple mechanism—a leather-covered box camera, pre-loaded with a roll of unexposed film. When the user had taken one hundred shots, they sent the camera back to the factory. For "only" $10 (about $290 today), the camera was returned, with a new roll of unexposed film installed, along with negatives and mounted prints. It was the old razors-and-razorblades model: sell customers an inexpensive device and make your money with the consumables it needs in order to work!

For many decades, Kodak was the undisputed North American giant of personal, professional, and industrial photography—based on its mastery of film and the devices used to control it. At times, it would do battle with its European and Asian counterparts (Agfa and Fujifilm), but the *status quo* remained essentially the same. However, with the advent of digital photography, computer-based imaging, and the web, everything changed.

It's popular to say that digital photography caught Kodak by surprise, but the reality is more complicated.[24] Kodak actually developed the first handheld digital camera in the mid-1970s, but quickly abandoned the project out of fear it would erode its film business. Despite this fear, the company later partnered with Apple and others to release its own very expensive digital cameras in 1996.

In the 1990s and early 2000s, Kodak acquired many new technologies and the companies who owned them, seemingly pursuing a version of an extender strategy. However, few if any of these acquisitions had anything to do with big data or AI—or so a casual observer might think. In reality, Kodak missed a gigantic opportunity to become a multiplier business.

In 2001, Kodak acquired Ofoto, a California-based startup that allowed users to upload, share, and print digital photographs. According to Scott Anthony at *Harvard Business Review*,[25] the purchase seemed to be a prescient one. The company had built its brand around the idea of sharing "Kodak Moments," and so it had a golden opportunity to leverage that into a social sharing site for pictures, personal events, news, and information—years before Facebook appeared on the social media scene.

To that mountain of unstructured data, Kodak could have applied real data science—and eventually artificial intelligence—to transform its business model, perhaps even becoming the leading social media platform. Unfortunately, the company chose instead to use it primarily for photo printing, a throwback to its original, nineteenth century business model. But users had moved on from printing photos to sharing them online, creating an avalanche of unstructured data that few companies saw as valuable. Kodak eventually sold the service as part of its 2012 bankruptcy reorganization.

The company has not fared well since it emerged from bankruptcy, but its financial troubles were not new ones. In 2010, six years after it had been removed from the Dow Jones Industrial Average, it was dropped from the S&P 500,[26] ending its fifty-three-year run as one of the 500 largest US companies.

Kodak's fall and Netflix's rise provide an important contrast. Kodak focused on the *product* (cameras, film, and later digital images) rather than the products' *value* to consumers.[27] As we saw in chapter 1, Netflix was willing to abandon their current product and follow the value—wherever the data told them it would be.

Taking Steps

As we will explore in part two, there are constructive ways to begin the journey into AI and big data. In a nutshell, here are the steps that companies need to follow:

- **Step One:** Look at your industry as a whole and identify the value points, weaknesses, or opportunities that no one else is exploiting. For Netflix, it was the difference between sending out DVDs versus streaming content.

- **Step Two:** Identify the limitations of your current business model—the things that prevent you from exploiting that hidden value.

- **Step Three:** Identify and understand the technologies that could unlock that value. (Re-read chapter 2 if necessary.)

- **Step Four:** Develop technology-based strategies to unlock that value. Remember that trying to do everything at once will probably not work, but always know what might be done next.

- **Step Five:** Implement those strategies to disrupt your business model. Remember that technical allies may get you there faster than going it alone.

- **Step Six:** Implement organizational and cultural solutions that will sustain change and keep your new business model evolving. Very often, the data and AI-driven insights themselves will serve as road markers, informing you of areas that still need change.

Following these steps is within the abilities of nearly every company or nonprofit. This is true even if the nature of your organization dictates starting with an optimizer or extender strategy. As the examples in this chapter illustrate, implementing AI does not require acting alone or having unlimited resources before you begin. There are always capable partners to help you start that journey—preferably with just one initiative at a time.

By starting to implement AI and big data, your business will be headed towards the same destination as Domino's or L'Oréal. If you do, you'll be ready to leave behind old business models, find and follow the data, and multiply your own intrinsic value.

Before moving on to the practical steps of planning and implementing an AI strategy, however, a cautionary note is warranted. Artificial intelligence, machine learning, and all their related technologies are created by human beings. And because we are human—and therefore flawed—the results of technology are sometimes imperfect as well. So, to create the best results—in *every* sense of the word—the following chapter will deal with the need to apply these tools in an ethical and responsible way.

CHAPTER 4

Ethical and Sustainable AI

In the fall of 2021, investigative journalists at the *Wall Street Journal* launched a devastating sixteen-part series exposing the unsavory practices of tech giant Facebook.[1] The articles and accompanying podcasts elicited strong public outcries and calls for regulation. The company responded primarily through PR initiatives and by changing the company name to Meta. However, as of this writing, it has not addressed the real problem: the unethical and irresponsible use of big data and artificial intelligence.

Using artificial intelligence-related technology in an unethical manner has real-world consequences. By the time you read this, Facebook (Meta) may be experiencing such consequences, including criminal or civil liability, increased regulation, and antitrust lawsuits, according to a report in *Brown Political Review*.[2] But there are also consequences for *all* companies and organizations, not just the giant tech companies like Facebook. Business ethics—which includes the ethical use of technology—has a significant impact on the bottom line, including greater returns for those who are ethical and declines in customer loyalty for those who are not.[3]

In other words, AI and big data can not only multiply your business success—as this book will help you realize. If used irresponsibly and unethically, they can multiply your business *failure.* They can also have tremendous effects—positive and negative—on people, on communities, and on the planet where you do business.

Technology is always like that. The late NYU professor Neil Postman famously noted the fallacy of assuming that technological innovation is one-sided in its effects. He said, "Every technology is both a burden and a blessing; not either-or, but this-and-that."[4] This is true of artificial intelligence.

The real difference with AI is speed. With earlier technologies, like printing, the steam engine, or automobiles, it took decades or longer to realize the results, both good and bad. But with AI, the results are close to instantaneous. By definition, AI and machine learning can discern patterns and make decisions faster than humans or their agencies can easily control. That's fine if the results are good for everyone, but not when they inevitably result in harm. With such a "combustible" technology, ethics and long-term sustainability are not just moral decisions. For business, they are imperatives.

What Is Ethical AI?

Because AI has such far-reaching potential, its ethical issues have been the subject of much academic study. A University of Tübingen paper analyzed *twenty-two* different AI ethics guidelines issued in the past five years.[5] But fortunately, others have distilled the subject into five basic principles:[6]

- **Transparency.** This includes several factors, including the requirement that an autonomous decision-making AI system must provide satisfactory explanations, auditable by a competent human authority. Also, if an AI causes harm, it should always be possible to ascertain why. AI is not a mysterious "black box." That popular fallacy must be countered by clearly making its actions understood.

- **Justice and Fairness.** This requires that highly autonomous AI systems be designed and operated in accordance with human values. It must be compatible with such ideals as human dignity and autonomy, basic rights, and respect for racial, gender, and cultural diversity. Bias in AI has become an unfortunate reality today,[7] especially when it comes to things like education, hiring, and credit applications. However, there are now concerted efforts to counter these biases in AI systems.[8]

- **Non-Maleficence.** AI systems must never be designed with a lethal or destructive purpose in mind. They should not only be safe and secure, but they should also be designed to benefit and empower as many people as possible. This includes the goal of shared economic prosperity, which will ultimately benefit both individuals and businesses across the globe. Non-maleficence also means that AI systems should be designed and used to respect and improve vital social and civic processes—not subvert them.

- **Responsibility.** This means that those who design, build, and use AI systems have a practical stake in their use, misuse, and results. They have a responsibility (and an opportunity) to control those uses and outcomes. This extends beyond the lifespan of any one individual or company. AI has the potential to profoundly change life on earth for the better, and to introduce catastrophic risks. Therefore, it imposes the need to manage the technology with great care and resources, and to plan and mitigate against bad outcomes.

- **Privacy and Choice.** Given the power and speed of AI to analyze personal data, the humans who generated the data should always have the right to access, manage, and control it. Also, when applied to personal data, AI must never unreasonably limit an individual's liberty—whether real or perceived. Privacy and autonomy also mean that humans should choose how (and whether) to delegate decisions to AI in accomplishing their human-chosen objectives.

The ethical implications of AI and big data have already been felt in terms of legal liability and risk mitigation.[9] Government regulation is typically slow in coming, but civil lawsuits—especially in the areas of bias, data security, personal privacy, and malicious acts by third parties—are expected to rise.[10] Risk managers are aware of the problem but less sure of the solution. In 2019, according to Accenture, 58 percent of those surveyed saw AI as the biggest potential cause of unintended consequences, but only 11 percent said they were fully capable of assessing those risks.[11] The Accenture study goes on to define four major "pillars" of responsible AI, including:

- **Organizational.** With support from leadership, companies should raise awareness of AI's risk potential, prioritize its long-term benefits over short-term product success, recognize the need for new performance metrics and roles, and actively upskill or hire for those roles.

- **Operational.** Companies and organizations should review and make their governance structures more transparent and more cross-domain by clearly identifying roles, expectations, and accountabilities when it comes to AI.

- **Technical.** AI systems should be designed to be fair, trustworthy, and explainable. This includes investing time in understanding bias and other factors effecting outcomes.

- **Reputational.** This involves not only adhering to a responsible business mission but also committing to ongoing
measurement of key responsible AI metrics to ensure they
are managing risk and communicating results clearly.

Ethical Frameworks Alone Are Not Enough

The ethical implications of AI and big data are formidable. To
protect their citizens, countries are beginning to enact laws and
regulations on their use, especially when it comes to privacy.
However, the unchecked use of AI in other countries may easily
affect citizens and businesses where it is regulated. This has led
many to advocate for establishing a set of international practices.[12]

There is no shortage of material to support this ideal. In 2020,
the Director of the Centre for Computing and Social Responsibility published a comprehensive book on the subject.[13] In 2021,
member states in the United Nations Educational, Scientific and
Cultural Organization (UNESCO) adopted the first global agreement on AI ethics.[14] The same year, the World Economic Forum
issued a human resources "toolkit" for implementing AI in an
ethical manner.[15] However, merely having these ideals in writing
is not enough. Businesses and organizations must establish clear
metrics and mechanisms for accountability in their planned use
of AI. And must do so *proactively* rather than waiting to measure
the harmful effects of AI after they happen.[16] Failing to act proactively will be more difficult and costly to a business' reputation,
their customers, and their bottom lines.

The Business Case

Studies indicate that business ethics in general are a critical
aspect of a company's or organization's long-term success.[17] And
because AI and big data produce results so rapidly, the ethical
mandate is even more important.

However, when it comes to ethical AI, taking a primarily *defensive* position does not tell the whole story. Companies and associations who take *proactively* ethical AI measures not only avoid costly lawsuits or government penalties. They also realize greater results—including financial ones. Think about your own loyalty to a brand whose AI-powered recommendation engine actually meets a need or makes your life easier. Now, think about how that loyalty would increase if you were confident in the brand's fairness and transparency—and respect for your privacy. A company that uses AI this way can only profit from such loyalty. Speaking to this issue in the *Harvard Business Review*, authors Greg Satell and Yassmin Abdel-Magied noted:[18]

> **"We need to start looking at eliminating AI bias less as merely 'a nice thing to do,' and more as an economic and competitive imperative. Business leaders take note: By making our AI systems more fair, we can also make our organizations more profitable and productive."**

As companies and other entities realize the enormous multiplier potential of AI and big data, they will be *intrinsically* motivated to apply it in an ethical and ultimately sustainable manner. In fact, it would not be surprising if companies and organizations—perhaps even governments—began to use AI itself to discover new ways to deploy AI and big data more ethically.

This is already happening in the healthcare field, where AI has the potential to add about thirteen trillion euros to the worldwide economy in 2030.[19] Already governed by established and enforceable medical ethics, as well as strict patient privacy requirements, healthcare is a natural fit for ethical AI. For example, in the US, Medicare claims constitute a huge data set. By definition (and by law), these data must be treated with extreme confidentiality. But when used ethically, they represent a rich source of predictive value for AI-driven business decisions.

Another promising area for ethical AI is in the realm of talent management. In the post-COVID-19 job market, demand for talent likely will continue to exceed supply, so companies will need the help of artificial intelligence to find the right people vital to their growth. But if the data set is skewed by gender or cultural bias, then the AI may only exacerbate the problems of hiring bias. In fact, some AI-driven hiring mechanisms will likely tempt employers to unfairly consider a candidate's race, sexual orientation, lifestyle, or disability (especially in countries with poor privacy protection) above their actual qualifications.[20] In the end, this may prevent companies from finding qualified people.

A 2019 *Harvard Business Review* article summarized the dilemma—and the potential solution.[21] Although AI use in talent management is still in its infancy, it has enormous potential to not only counteract bias but also augment the association between talent, effort, and employee success. If the big data set included more objective and rigorous *performance* metrics—and fewer subjective and typically biased assessments—then AI would be more likely to find matches based on merit alone. It says that AI can mirror existing behavior, including undue bias in HR hiring practices, but that better AI results can be achieved by addressing bias in the underlying training data set.

AI and big data are already competitive differentiators for many companies, including those who combine responsibility and ethics with dramatic multipliers in cost savings and profit.[22] They include Aclima's cloud-based platform to turn big data on air quality into actionable hyperlocal insights and Snowflake's AI approach to tackling multiple business challenges. (Snowflake's 2020 initial public offering was the biggest in software history, and the company is still going strong.[23]) In partnership with McGill University and others, AI developer Theator analyzed thousands of hours of surgical videos to provide knowledgeable feedback to surgeons and surgeons in training. A study concluded that integrating AI systems in surgical workflows would assist in the decision-making process, ultimately improving the surgeon experience and patient care.[24]

The AI solution need not be overly complex or expensive. Any business or organization can find ways to fix broken systems and solve complex problems. A great example of doing both is best illustrated by a nonprofit animal shelter organization:[25]

Founded in 1984, the Best Friends Animal Society's ambition mission was to end the killing of healthy adoptable animals in shelters by 2025. It had partnered with over 3,000 shelters and rescue organizations, and with about 10,000 animal-related partners overall. Its challenge was to turn massive amounts of data from pet owners, veterinarians, groomers, and other sources into actionable intelligence—allowing shelters and rescue organizations to easily trace and find an animal's owner or suitable prospective owner.

By working with developers like Vendia and Magvii, and using low-cost cloud data services from Amazon's AWS, the Society is creating a blockchain-based data network called Pet Chain. By using this tamper-proof system, animals can be followed throughout their lifespan, and AI algorithms can use the data to identify and reunite lost animals easily.

Their use of data had improved on the Society's already impressive "no-kill" record—a 96 percent reduction in the number of animals killed in shelters. Even more impressive is the relative ease with which the solution was achieved. "The cherry on top for me is that a nonprofit with barely any specialized developers can do this in a pretty straightforward way," said Vendia co-founder. "If a nonprofit can use cutting-edge technology with minimal to no developer profile in their companies, anyone can."

The Best of Both Worlds?

When it comes to AI, big data, and smart devices, the idea of combining profitability and ethics can perhaps best be illustrated in the case of another somewhat smaller coffee company, Coda Coffee:[26]

In 2005, Tim and Tommy Thwaites founded Coda, a coffee roaster and wholesaler in Denver, Colorado. Among its founding principles was a dedication to producing high-quality coffee while protecting the environment and promoting sustainable farming practices. That meant working directly with farmers and paying them a premium for the best coffee beans.

About 25 million smallholder farmers account for approximately 80 percent of the world's coffee production. They own small plots of land and rely mainly on family labor to produce a cash crop. Fair Trade certification, first introduced in 1988, was established as a means of fairly compensating these small farmers while also benefiting them by introducing and promoting sustainable farming practices.

The Thwaites saw the benefits of fair trade but knew there were limitations when it came to guaranteeing bean quality. "Fair Trade certifications have a floor for their coffee quality," they said, "so without an outside party going the farm and pushing these coffee growers to grow better coffee, there can be little incentive to go above that quality floor."

So, in 2011, the company introduced a more ambitious certification program, Farm2Cup, where farmers would receive significantly better prices for their coffee, so long as it met certain quality standards achievable through better and more sustainable farming practices. (The program also encouraged farmers to give back to their communities in other ways, often supported by independent contributions by Coda.)

The problem was that bean quality measurement was primarily a subjective visual perception process—one that would not easily

73

scale Coda's business. Because hiring more experts to judge bean quality was not an option, AI was the logical answer.

Coda Coffee then partnered with Bext360, developers of a device that combined visual detection and AI to determine the characteristics of large quantities of physical objects—in this case, coffee beans. In the pilot study in Uganda, every coffee bean was imaged and, using AI, analyzed for color, brightness, and defects. A resulting "cupping score" of over eighty points indicated the coffee was Specialty Grade, for which the farmer was given a receipt for immediate payment.

For each batch, from the point the beans were processed by the machine, the AI component provided a text file to the cloud, where it became a secure blockchain record. At each step in the coffee production process, a new and immutable blockchain record would be added to the chain, providing complete transparency between the Ugandan point of origin to Coda Coffee in Denver.

Not only did AI provide a way to automate the quality evaluation process, and incentivize farmers in the process, it also gave Coda Coffee the means of multiplying their visionary business.

In 2019, Coda was on track to grow by 20 to 30 percent, year over year.[27] Not bad for a company founded on ethical convictions that also used AI to live up to those convictions and make money in the process.

The Human Factor

Finally, one of the greatest ethical or sociological barriers to widespread adoption of AI and machine learning is the fear that the technology will eliminate jobs by automating repetitive or mundane tasks. While it's true that many tasks will be handled more efficiently using AI, many of those tasks are ones that humans were already ill-equipped to perform in the first place. Think about Netflix's approach to image analysis—judging which of movie thumbnail images "A" or "B" got better results. In theory, human beings could have performed that analysis manually, but the time and expense would have been enormous. That high cost was why no one had seriously attempted it before and why Netflix's doing it with AI and machine learning (ML) was so revolutionary.

No one can deny that automation has disrupted the workforce *status quo*—as it has done since the Industrial Revolution. Jobs performed manually will always be subject to radical change and a certain amount of pain. But this argument ignores the potential of the AI Factor to create new jobs and, more importantly, enhance the effectiveness of existing jobs performed by human beings.

One of the most notable examples of this is occurring at Levi Strauss & Company, the 170-year-old company best known as the inventor of blue jeans. Led by Chief Global Strategy and AI Officer Katia Walsh, the company's digital initiatives include a wide range of business improvements, including an AI-powered process for new product design. In a recent *Me, Myself, and AI* podcast episode,[28] Walsh described the company's new "machine learning boot camps," where employees work with data scientists to develop new AI solutions and become even more aware of the role of data in their own jobs.

> Speaking of the 101 graduates attending boot camps as of this writing, Walsh noted, "We had about 450 applications. This is not a program for everyone, because it takes people out of their day job for eight weeks." The results have been remarkable—for both the company and for its employees, many of whom have applied their new skills to everyday job situations. Bootcamp graduates have applied their new skills to a range of areas throughout the company, from automating supply chain reporting to creating predictive maintenance models for distribution centers, optimizing store location selection, and helping transform demand prediction.

Bootcamp graduates have also helped Levi Strauss move forward in the realm of product design. "Humans are actually the most important part of artificial intelligence," Walsh said, "whether it's human-centric design, or it's humans that are making machines smarter. And of course in turn, machines help us become even better. In the case of AI-powered design, what is even more fascinating is that this work at Levi's was pioneered by one of our young designers who had no formal training in machine learning or computer science. He's one of the 101 graduates of our industry-first machine learning boot camp."

An important benefit of this approach is greatly enhanced retention of valuable employees. "Most of the people who graduate from the boot camp go back to their roles," Walsh said. "There are people who want to become very advanced data scientists and, of course, we don't want to deprive them of that opportunity, and we do give them that opportunity when the time comes. But the vast majority stay in their existing roles and thus upgrade their own roles."

Levi Strauss is a leader among the many companies employing the AI Factor to become a multiplier business, as we will explore in greater detail in part two. But perhaps the thing that most distinguishes them is their emphasis on the most important part of the sustainability equation: people.[29] While ethical issues such as transparency, fairness, and privacy are critical factors, the ultimate test of an enduring data strategy is whether it values and supports human beings and the planet on which they live.

The Best Path Forward

Ethical and sustainable AI is always possible, although never guaranteed. Like every technology from the wheel and fire to the printing press and beyond, data science can be used for bad purposes as well as good ones. But the likelihood of using it for good—and for greater long-term financial benefit—increases when we recall Katia Walsh's words:

*"Humans are actually the most important part
of artificial intelligence."*

So the big question is, if AI can be applied in an ethical and sustainable manner, and if doing so is both affordable and capable of creating a business multiplier effect, then why are more companies not doing so? In part two, we'll explore the practical steps that can differentiate your company or organization from the rest of the pack—and multiply your success.

PART TWO

APPLYING
THE AI FACTOR

A Voyage of Self-Discovery

As a data strategy consultant, I have encountered numerous companies and their leaders struggling to incorporate the AI Factor into their day-to-day operations. The same holds true for many members of the peer-to-peer mastermind organization I founded and have the honor to lead.* We each have stories—about our own companies and about those we advise. Some of those are included this book, with permission, but others are understandably too confidential to share here.

So, to illustrate the principles contained in the next four chapters, I will share the story of a fictional company and its successful use big data and AI. While the narrative is fictional, it represents a composite of real-world examples of business and nonprofit exploits I have witnessed over the years.

• — •

---

* Women Leaders in Data and AI (WLDA); https://wlda.tech.

Founded in the early-2000s, "Octothorpe Unlimited"
was a typical regional startup company hoping to
expand across the country. From the start, the company resold high-end, high-quality, specialty food
products—"by the pound"—directly to restaurants and catering
companies. (The name comes from a 1970s word for the pound
sign.) They had achieved annual sales of around $50 million, but,
faced with growing competition from traditional food wholesalers,
Octothorpe management realized they needed to do something
differently. The rise of social media (and the coincidental popularity of their corporate symbol, the hashtag) made a data-driven
AI solution seem like the right move. But like many other companies, they did not know where to begin.

The first step was to acquire a clear understanding of their
own growth potential and their willingness to take risks. Was
their basic business position a defensive one, mainly looking to
cut costs and increase efficiency? Were they looking to acquire
new customers or develop new products? Or were they willing to
be audacious—willing to discard old business models and reinvent new ones?

After some intensive brainstorming and self-reflection, their
position became clear. As a somewhat new tech-savvy company,
Octothorpe was clearly not defending a status quo. Greater efficiency would be nice, they thought, but the key desire was **to
extend or enlarge their base** to new customers—perhaps even to
new customer types, not just restaurants and caterers.

As chapter 5 will explain, Octothorpe's business position—
that of an "extender"—is one of four different types. Each of these
can apply the power of the AI Factor to achieve their immediate
goals. They may also do so in order to fundamentally change the
type of business they are, ultimately becoming a multiplier business and achieving exponential growth.

CHAPTER 5

Assessing Your Business

At this point, you have a better understanding of the transformative potential of artificial intelligence and its related technologies. But the bigger questions still remain: "What can I do? We're not Netflix and I'm not Reed Hastings! How can I possibly implement AI *now*? It's too much! How do I even start?"

These are fair questions. As we saw in chapter 2, there are many popular misconceptions about AI—and lots of fear and uncertainty. Even if you know better or have been encouraged by the examples in part one, your colleagues and employees may take some convincing.

This chapter (and the next three) will detail the stages or steps you need to take in order to implement AI and big data successfully. For reference, these stages are:

- **ASSESS:** Identifying the inherent growth and innovation potential of your business, and the potential benefits of data-driven strategies for each type of business.

- **FRAME:** Understanding and assessing your company's organizational maturity and internal competence—factors that determine its overall data-readiness.
- **PRIORITIZE:** Selecting and pursuing the business goal with the highest potential business value that can be met using AI and its related technologies.
- **MEASURE:** Tracking not only the scientific results but also the business changes resulting from data-driven projects—to ensure that they gain traction beyond the immediate goal and transform the business itself.

Throughout this process, it's important to remember that data science is simply that—a science, one that uses empirical methods, processes, and systems to derive knowledge from both structured and unstructured data. It can be used for good purposes or bad, as we discussed in chapter 4, but it does not have a mind of its own. It is also not the exclusive domain of large corporations. The purpose of this book is to help you prove otherwise—that almost anyone can utilize AI effectively to achieve remarkable results.

Growth Assessment

The first stage of this process is to understand your business' current potential for growth. There are many ways to do this, of course, and most executives do it on a regular basis, using tools such as the familiar business model canvas shown here.

This "vision board" approach provides an at-a-glance overview of what a company hopes to be in a year, five years, or longer. It's far more than a business modeling tool, however. It outlines a coherent general business strategy including potential trade-offs. As we'll see, it can also inform the data-driven initiatives that can support such a strategy.

For example, in 1999, Netflix's value proposition consisted of supplying unlimited rentals of DVD-based content to movie and

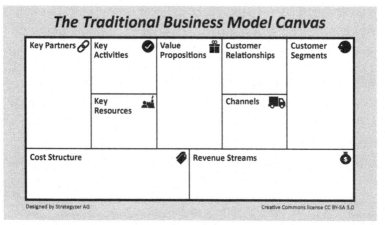

The Traditional Business Model Canvas

Key Partners	Key Activities	Value Propositions	Customer Relationships	Customer Segments
	Key Resources		Channels	

Cost Structure	Revenue Streams

Designed by Strategyzer AG — Creative Commons license CC BY-SA 3.0

Planning for business growth often starts with basic value propositions before defining target customer segments, delivery channels, and revenue streams. This will evolve over time, but ultimately every aspect of such a plan will dictate a company's data-driven initiatives.

TV consumers—with no due dates and no late fees. This in turn dictated a delivery channel (online ordering and home delivery) which provided a stable, subscription-based revenue stream.

That model was vulnerable to competition. More importantly, Netflix sought to understand their customers' needs, which shifted their value proposition to *content recommendation*—something that required a sophisticated analysis of big data. This drove the company's channel strategy to streaming content, even before streaming infrastructure was up to the task. This soon resulted in an acceleration of subscription revenue, and ultimately in new key activities—original content based on their content recommendation data.

With the help of big data and AI, a growth plan is an invaluable means of identifying ways to increase efficiencies and lower costs. It can also help identify new resources or partners. It can even identify potential new products or new breakthrough business models—or reinvent your business entirely. But before you can do any of those things, you need to know where your business stands.

Where You Stand Now—and What You Want to Be

Most companies have some idea of their basic value proposition and its implications, even without the business model canvas described above. But doing a growth assessment also forces us to look at the type of company we now are and, more importantly, what we want to become.

The next step in assessing your business and its best approach to big data and AI comes down to two important factors:

- *Your willingness to innovate and take risks,* even abandoning old business models and conventions in order to create new ones, and

- *The future growth potential* of the market or service area you are in.

These are the basis for the business model discussed earlier in chapter 1:

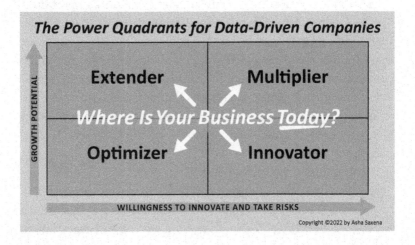

The Power Quadrants for Data-Driven Companies

GROWTH POTENTIAL

Extender   Multiplier

Where Is Your Business Today?

Optimizer   Innovator

WILLINGNESS TO INNOVATE AND TAKE RISKS

Copyright ©2022 by Asha Saxena

Every business is different, of course. But knowing where you stand at the moment is not difficult. Some companies, like those described in part one, are clearly in the multiplier category—fully prepared to innovate, take risks, and even bend the rules to realize that potential, as we'll explore later in the chapter. But what does that mean for other business types? Do you have to be a multiplier to use AI and big data effectively? As we will see in the next several chapters, the answer is *no*.

> *No matter how innovative, daring, or growth-driven your company may be, AI and big data have enormous potential benefits and can lead you to greater growth and innovation.*

Being a multiplier company—one whose growth and value increases exponentially—is a likely *result* of using data effectively, not a requirement for doing so. In fact, companies that implement AI within the limitations of their own organization are more likely to change and grow. By following the data deliberately, with the help of AI and supporting technologies, they may start out as one type of company but ultimately become a multiplier. It's true that they will have to make changes and unlearn old habits. But in doing so, they can multiply their success beyond all expectations.

Before describing each of the four quadrants, and how companies in each one can benefit from AI, we need to understand their defining vectors—innovation/risk-taking and the potential for growth.

The Dynamics of Innovation

Innovation may seem like a subjective notion, but there are ways to look at it objectively. A 2006 report described the measurable relationship between innovation and business performance, in terms of sales growth, market share, and profitability.[1] The report surveyed both manufacturing and service-oriented companies, showing the positive results for companies that innovated either their product offerings, their processes, or both.

A Kennesaw State University report defined innovation as something that "takes place when management is willing to *change the company's business model* (emphasis added) to capitalize on new ideas" at the time they believe those ideas are ready to be implemented.[2] The report found that innovation-driven companies shared common characteristics, including:

- *A high level of involvement by CEOs and other executives* as drivers of innovation initiatives,
- *Incentives, hiring policies, and budget allocations* that reward and encourage a culture of innovation,
- *Open communication practices* that reduce the fear of risk-taking, and
- *Reliable metrics* for business initiatives that not only show what happened and why but also predict what will happen and how to make good outcomes more likely.

Other business books rightly focus on the first innovation indicators, executive leadership, incentives, hiring, budgets, and open communication. While these are important, the last factor—reliable metrics—is of particular interest for implementing big data and AI. By applying *and measuring* these technologies in a reliable, meaningful way, companies and nonprofits are fueling their potential to innovate.

Finally, a company's willingness to take risks is directly related to their capacity for product and process innovation. Whether that innovation is disruptive or incremental, if a company or nonprofit is reluctant to challenge "the way we've always done things," then it is likely to suffer the consequences. Recall the fate of a company formerly known for its innovation—Eastman Kodak—described in chapter 3. Contrast that company's risk aversion with rival Xerox, whose service innovation approach saved it from suffering Kodak's fate.[3] The two companies' recent history proved the truism that "Innovation is risky... But what's really risky is not innovating."[4]

Fortunately, a company's willingness to innovate does not prevent it from implementing AI and big data, as we will see. In the long run, however, innovation will always be a hallmark of companies that excel at using data to multiply their value over the long haul.

Limits to Growth, Real and Imagined

The second vector used to determine a company's position in the four quadrants is its potential for growth. Like innovation, growth potential can be a tricky concept. Perhaps the demand for a company's product or service really has peaked, and there are literally no new markets to conquer. If a company's sole focus was on making buggy whips or fax machines, or if it offered equally obsolete services, then its growth potential will obviously be nil. When a market becomes truly saturated or when product demand stagnates, such companies don't last long. They are shut down, acquired, or (in a best case scenario) transformed into something else. That is why it is necessary to constantly evaluate thought data and metrics—to discover where the need for change exists.

The point is that limits to growth are often in the minds of those who fail to see new opportunities. Just as risk aversion stifles innovation, narrow thinking limits a company's ability to grow past its current model.

While the potential for growth is often linked to innovation of *new product ideas*, there are other ways to expand one's growth potential and fuel business expansion.[5] These include:

- **Acquiring new business capabilities** through M&A or part-nerships. While not as glamorous as inventing the latest in disruptive technology, M&A is a valid choice for company growth. Today, it is also frequently optimized by artificial intelligence.

- **Developing new processes** for offering the same products or services at higher margins. This often involves cut-ting production costs, automation efficiencies, and other improvements made possible by (you guessed it) artificial intelligence and robotics.

- **Acquiring new customers** for existing products and ser-vices by using big data and AI to develop marketing and sales "funnel" strategies that actually connect with users' preferences and purchase behavior. Of course, it is possible to develop a customer acquisition plan without utilizing AI; it's just a lot harder to succeed that way. (Marketing depart-ments and agencies are littered with SEO, branding, and loyalty-building campaigns that rely more on gut feelings than data science.)

- **Utilizing new channels** for selling or distributing your prod-ucts. When it comes to digital commerce, re-inventing the wheel is not necessary. There are many options for ecom-merce automation available to streamline the process. Of course, many of these were developed by companies in the multiplier quadrant (see below) but that does not preclude you from using them.

The potential for business growth is subject to many factors outside our control, including employment fluctuations, market conditions, and other "macro" influences.[6] However, there are many things a company *can* do in order to grow.

Your willingness to innovate and your ability to grow determine which of the four quadrants best describes your company. No combination prevents you from implementing big data and AI successfully, but knowing where you stand will help you determine the best possible way to do so. But before you attempt to identify your company's position, let's summarize the four quadrants themselves.

Optimizer Companies

Companies in this quadrant can be of any size or age but the term is often associated with relatively large well-established firms. Inherently cautious and conservative by nature, such companies tend to focus on bottom-line cost savings, optimizing the process efficiency, reducing potential liability, and protecting their intellectual property. While these things are all good business practices, they can indicate a company's aversion to risk and change as well as a perception—true or not—that there is limited potential for growth.

Cost cutting—one of the hallmarks of optimizer companies—is not without the risk of harmful long-term results.[7] On one hand, if the aim is to maintain or improve product or service quality, then wise cost cutting is an obvious move. (It is also a prime opportunity to employ customer and service data via artificial intelligence algorithms.) However, cost reduction—especially workforce reduction—is often done for short-term balance sheet reasons, with disastrous consequences. The immediate financial savings are more than overcome by declining employee trust and interest in the company's success—and ultimately in declining customer trust and loyalty. Ironically, properly deployed big data and AI would have predicted such a result, and guided the company in making different cost cutting decisions.

The good news for optimizer companies is that AI can be extremely effective in strengthening operational efficiency, customer service, and other areas that typify companies with less perceived growth potential and less willingness to innovate and take risks.

How exactly does AI help optimizer companies? It can do so, for example, by harnessing their *existing* data, such as its customer preferences, their purchase behavior, and the company's service history. AI and big data can lower operational costs, reduce errors, strengthen customer loyalty, and minimize or even eliminate financial decline. In time, it may also lead the company to realize new business opportunities or product ideas that would elevate it to the extender or innovator categories. It may even lead to becoming an outlier company, capable of multiplied growth *and* innovation.

Extender Companies

In markets where potential growth is obvious, but the company is wary of risk or change, the extender strategy is very common. Tried and true manufacturing or service methods are in place, and the company has achieved success in its existing sphere. What distinguishes extender from optimizer companies is an overwhelming desire or mandate to grow—to conquer new worlds, so long as the new worlds look much like the current ones.

By far the most common method of achieving such growth is through M&A, both of rival companies and of those whose products or services may resemble their own. M&A is sometimes referred to as *inorganic* growth, as opposed to the organic process of innovation and product development described later in the chapter. The key objective—greater market share—is accomplished simply by gaining the customers of the acquired rival and selling those new customers the same products or services under a new brand. If the acquired company happens to be more willing to take risks and create new products, then the acquiring company may reap the benefits of being an innovator company (see below) without taking the risks involved.

Growth via M&A can also be hazardous. The Harvard Business School defined four major risk factors, including the lack of due diligence, overpayment, misguided notions about the value of the proposed combination, and unforeseen difficulties in combining operations and company cultures.[8] In a 2016 survey of senior finance professionals, miscalculations about the acquired company's value and its operations topped the list of fifteen causes for concern that resulted in financial loss.[9]

The application of AI can be of enormous benefit here. When considering a merger (combining two companies into a new entity) or an acquisition, there are enormous quantities of data available to both parties. This includes both structured (think spreadsheets and databases) and unstructured data. M&A teams typically focus on the former. What was the revenue for the past ten years? What were the costs for the same period? How did each product group or service category grow or decline over time?

Such structured data can provide a basic "skeleton" picture of the company to be acquired, but little more than that. Very often, the missing details about a company's true value and operations are filled in by the experience or "gut instincts" of the principals or their advisors. This common but unscientific approach often results in overvaluing the acquisition or missing an important business flaw, which in turn can lead to poor results.

In 2003, a *Harvard Business Review* article noted that reliance on intuition may *seem* necessary, because of the rapid increase in the volume of data and the narrowing of available time to analyze it.[10] However, the same article also points out that the subconscious process we call intuition can be fatally flawed. It is subject to confirmation bias (preferring evidence that supports what we already believe), sunk cost fallacies, framing, and other cognitive biases described by Nobel prize winner Daniel Kahneman in his landmark book *Thinking, Fast and Slow*.[11] The same *HBR* article (from almost twenty years ago) predicted a better solution:

> Technology may hold the key. Sophisticated computer programs are now being developed that can supplement and bolster people's decision-making skills. Many of these new decision-support tools are still in the early stages of development and have yet to be applied to strategic business decisions. But they hold enormous potential for helping executives carry out the two key components of decision-making or problem-solving exercises: *searching* for possible solutions and *evaluating* those solutions in order to choose the best one or ones. The more complex and fast-changing the situation, the more challenging both search and evaluation become. By expanding the analytical as well as the intuitive capabilities of the mind, the new programs allow a much faster, a much fuller, and a much more rigorous exploration of the options.

This observation clearly indicates a data-driven process—one that can only be accomplished via artificial intelligence and machine learning. For M&A purposes, the right AI analysis of unstructured data would provide greater insights into a potential acquisition's true value, and even offer reliable predictions of its future performance potential.

Today, big data and AI are becoming an integral part of the M&A process. According to a KPMG Australia report, buyers are increasingly using quantitative predictive insights over qualitative ones to support their value hypotheses.[12] For attorneys during the due diligence phase, AI is proving to be a cost-saving boon, accelerating the review process, and creating greater budget certainty.[13]

●——————●

Another characteristic of extender companies is an emphasis on greater marketing efforts, both for their existing products or services and for those of any acquired entities. It is always difficult to create a compelling brand message for a large, diverse set of deliverables, but it is essential in order to retain and expand a company's market share and top line revenue. Companies in this quadrant may not have a strong desire to innovate, but they do know that new customer acquisition, retention, conversion, and brand loyalty are the keys to success.

Marketing initiatives can take many forms, of course. For many, today's marketing landscape contains far too many forms of communication. What was once a relatively simple task of advertising in publications, broadcast media, and on signs or in-store displays is now a bewildering array of media channels. To name only a few: these include websites that always need fresh content, endless social media feeds, surveys, and direct online interaction with customers. Topping it all off are the endless streams of unstructured data coming from all these channels.

That last sentence will give you a hint about the likely solution for extender companies and their marketing campaigns. By utilizing artificial intelligence and big data effectively, companies can find meaningful patterns that are all but impossible to detect manually. Knowing these patterns of likely customer behavior will inform decisions on which channels and content are most effective in gaining attention, provoking interest and desire, and prompting meaningful action.

Marketing itself comes with inherent risks,[14] including declining brand awareness, misguided product development, and failure to anticipate actual demand. A University of West London study found a direct relationship between marketing and consumer trust. It also found a relationship to purchasing decisions and the risk to web vendors.[15] Obviously, all of these initiatives are a potential source of data—in addition to the company's existing customer data—which represent fertile ground for the use of artificial intelligence.

All of these risk factors can be anticipated and avoided when the available data are properly used. With the right application of AI, extender companies can approach both M&A and marketing efforts with a much greater likelihood of success.

Innovator Companies

The next quadrant—innovators—includes those aggressive risk-taking companies whose growth potential is not yet obvious, at least to the outside world. Typical, perhaps stereotypical examples of innovators include tech startups and entrepreneurs of almost every type and size. (It also includes "intrapreneurs," those individuals and groups within large companies who innovate internally.) Others include traditional service providers and manufacturers looking to transcend their existing offerings and broaden their customer base. An innovator's chief characteristics are ambition, vision, and a desire to change things for the better, even before their big ideas for products or services are proven successful.

Innovator strategies nearly always involve R&D. New products or services must be planned, designed, and tested—which is fertile potential ground for artificial intelligence and big data. By analyzing relevant unstructured data on consumer behavior and other factors, AI can more reliably predict the types of products and services that would meet people's needs, informing product developers and designers and giving them valid criteria for testing and subsequent promotion.

AI and big data are already significant aspects of R&D for pharmaceutical companies, not only helping with product design specifications but also with managing clinical trials, participant identification, and dosage error reduction.[16] It is also emerging in the industrial manufacturing sector, providing more objective identification of user requirements, better exploration of market trends, and higher product design efficiency.[17] All this points to an even larger trend:

> *"[Artificial intelligence] may have an even larger impact on the economy by serving as a new general-purpose 'method of invention' that can reshape the nature of the innovation process and the organization of R&D."*[18]

So, for innovator companies focused on aggressive R&D initiatives, AI and big data are imperative. Even companies with smaller IT budgets benefit from emerging third-party tools that will help them accurately quantify customer needs and identify, create, and test the resulting products and services.

•————•

Another chief characteristic of innovator companies is their equally aggressive pursuit of top talent, a difficult task made even more so by the disruptions of the COVID-19 pandemic. In a globalized, "sellers' market" for skilled employees, companies are often hard put to recruit the talent they need to develop and promote their new products and services. Once again, this is a prime opportunity for companies to use big data and AI.

The role of AI in today's hiring practices is well established—if sometimes controversial.[19] As we discussed in chapter 4, human bias can be present in AI algorithms, especially if the data set is not representative of the population as a whole or contains elements subject to misinterpretation. In 2018, Amazon famously had to discontinue its AI-enabled recruitment system because it could not stop the tool from discriminating against women.[20] This has prompted some analysts to declare that predictive AI tends to preserve the *status quo*, because they are based on inadequate or biased data sets.

As usual, the reality is more complicated. AI unquestionably decreases the time required to sort through resumes, freeing HR professionals to focus on more qualitative matters. But current recruiting AIs are vulnerable to human bias and to candidates trying to "game the system" by using known keywords. A recent *Forbes* article weighed these pros and cons, ultimately tasking HR and IT departments with the responsibility of thinking beyond minimum compliance requirements—monitoring the entire recruitment process for potential bias.[21]

Used wisely, however, AI can identify candidates that traditional recruitment may miss.[22] As an aid to recruiters looking for unorthodox or non-traditional skills and experience, it just may be what innovator companies need to find and hire the next atypical superstar.

Multiplier Companies

When a company or nonprofit knows its true growth potential and is fully prepared to innovate and take risks to realize that potential, then it will be one willing to bend the rules. Companies fitting this description are amply described in chapters one through four, so there is less need to describe them here.

Being a multiplier does not mean violating individual rights, or ethical norms, or exploiting others unfairly for financial gain. What I mean by rule-bending is a willingness to challenge the *status quo*, discarding old models and practices, transforming your business model from the ground up. Becoming a multiplier does not happen overnight, nor can you disguise reckless or destructive business practices under a multiplier label. Once you embrace a mentality of innovation and growth, however, the use of big data and AI will be a perfect fit.

This requires a certain level of audacity. Netflix decided to all but abandon its DVD rental model and embrace streaming—long before streaming was practical. The company's customer feedback data was abysmal from a PR perspective. But instead of handling it in the typical PR manner, the company embraced that data and used it to transform their business model. Coda Coffee was (and is) committed to the ethical principles of fair trade, which had limitations when it came to product quality incentives. But their willingness to take risks with AI and technology gave them a way to transform their business.

With the right combination of audacity and data science, you can become a multiplier business as well.

Once you have assessed the core nature of your business, you can move on to the next stage—knowing your company's "data readiness" capabilities, the subject of the next chapter.

Do You Have What It Takes?

Our fictional company, Octothorpe Unlimited, has achieved some success reselling high-end food products to restaurants and catering companies, but their growth was modest and they were vulnerable to competition. The company's CEO knew all this and was passionate about the latent potential of data and technology to improve her business. Clearly, there was executive buy-in, which is a key element of a company's "data readiness." But that enthusiasm alone was not enough.

For a new company, Octothorpe's organizational maturity was above average. They knew that with the right data, they would have a clear idea of what their current and potential future customers would need—and how to deliver it more efficiently. The company was also beginning to take a holistic approach to data management, adding feedback and preferences from ordering and service calls to every customer profile. Early on, they created cloud storage accounts for their data and started using various cloud services for ordering and invoicing. Overall data literacy was above average, especially among their digital marketing and IT people, both of whom were open to working with strategic partners. Overall, the company was well on its way to becoming a data-driven entity.

Chapter 6 lays out the two major pillars of a company's data readiness—their capacity to carry out and benefit exponentially from the AI Factor. The first pillar, organizational maturity, deals with a company's strategic and operational strengths and its standards for data management. The second pillar, internal competency, deals with a company's internal capacity to use data and its readiness to create scalable transformational data solutions. While no business can morph instantly into a data rock star, this chapter will serve as a roadmap for preparing you to leverage data and AI more effectively.

CHAPTER 6

Your Data-Readiness Framework

Once you've characterized your *business* readiness—your inherent or desired potential for growth and innovation—you must now uncover your company's or nonprofit's *data* readiness. Artificial intelligence may not be scary or malevolent, but it's still not easy.

To start with, to know if your business is ready for a data-driven strategy, you must actually *have* robust sources of relevant data, including both the structured and unstructured kind. The good news is that most companies have (or at least have access to) the data they need, whether they know it or not.

Data Basics

Many organizations have only a tenuous notion of what their data actually are—and what sources they have for collecting it. Capable IT departments naturally have a firm grasp of their *structured* transactional data, but it is often siloed in different databases and isolated in individual departments. The difficulty is in viewing data as a whole and in incorporating *unstructured* data into the mix.

There are a growing number of ways to collect more data, particularly the unstructured variety.[1] Traditional *active data collection* is simply the process of asking for it. In ascending order of difficulty, this includes surveys and questionnaires, focus groups, and interviews. Surveys can also provide a great deal of structured data if the questions are well designed. More recent forms of active data collection involve collecting unstructured data (text, images, and video) from social media and other sources. Known as "social listening" or "social sentiment analysis," this uses AI processes like NLP to parse huge volumes of data to determine the deeper context and meaning on a desired topic. AI thus becomes a silent listener for analyzing behavior and trends.

Another source is *passive or permissions-based data collection*. Recorded customer service calls or texts are a rich potential trove of such data—provided it is processed for significant meaning and trends using AI. Ecommerce activity is yet another example, where meaningful data can be gathered (hopefully with the user's consent) from browsing and purchasing decisions, geolocation, referrals, and product reviews, both positive and negative.

Directly adjacent to ecommerce is the customer loyalty program, ideally one that is integrated with the ordering experience. By offering discounts and specials, such a program can create a flood of valuable business data. Special care must be taken with such programs, not only to ensure data security but also to make sure the customer's privacy is not violated—even by implication.

In the early 2000s, data expert Andrew Pole devised a predictive model for the Target retail chain. Based on individual buying patterns, he could determine when a woman had become pregnant—even before she knew it herself. Because the company was able to customize its print and online promotions, Pole's data model enabled them to feature products of high interest to expectant mothers. However, the company also realized the "creepiness factor" of it knowing a woman's reproductive plans. So, it wisely refrained from advertising only those products.[2]

A third source is *public data collection*. This may be as simple as accessing public records, documents, or databases like Data. gov. These come with the caveat that they are general by definition and can be outdated.

Other ostensibly public data sources include social media sites—from posts and comments to images and video—which fall under the social listening form of active data collection described above. However, these data are typically controlled by the platform owners for their explicit commercial benefit. While there are ways for third parties to pay for and use this data, extreme caution is warranted. As the privacy backlash continues against social media, many are increasingly turning to a permissions-based approach.[3]

Yet another source of data for AI and ML use is the relatively recent phenomenon of *synthetic data* which will account for 60 percent of all data used in AI development by 2024, according to the Gartner Group.[4] Accenture data science and machine learning engineering lead Fernando Lucini defined this paradoxical concept in a 2021 *MIT Sloan Management Review* article:

"Synthetic data is artificially generated by an AI algorithm that has been trained on a real data set. It has the same predictive power as the original data but replaces it rather than disguising or modifying it. The goal is to reproduce the statistical properties and patterns of an existing data set by modeling its probability distribution and sampling it out. The algorithm essentially creates new data that has all of the same characteristics of the original data—leading to the same answers. However, crucially,

> it's virtually impossible to reconstruct the original data (think personally identifiable information) from either the algorithm or the synthetic data it has created."[5]

This is a potential boon for AI projects, since it replaces private data, such as personal medical or financial information, eliminating the need to anonymize. However, it is far from perfect, as Lucini himself cautioned.

> "We are just in the beginning stages of creating the tools, frameworks, and metrics needed to assess and 'guarantee' the accuracy of synthetic data. Getting to an industrialized, repeatable approach is critical to creating accurate synthetic data via a standard process that's accepted and trusted by everyone."

The privacy-versus-utility argument is also not settled. A study prepared for the 2022 USENIX Security Symposium concluded that "synthetic data is far from the holy grail of privacy-preserving data publishing."[6]

The Data-Readiness Framework

In chapter 5, we discussed ways to assess your businesses' potential for growth and innovation. The resulting business model canvas typically contains a concise version of your immediate and long-term business goals. Once that and an adequate source of data are established, the next step is to connect the two. This is not a "once-and-done" process. Every data-centric strategy and project should be thoroughly evaluated according to the company's *organizational maturity* as well as its *internal competence* when it comes to data use. Think of these as two pillars supporting your company's goal to achieve exponential business growth.

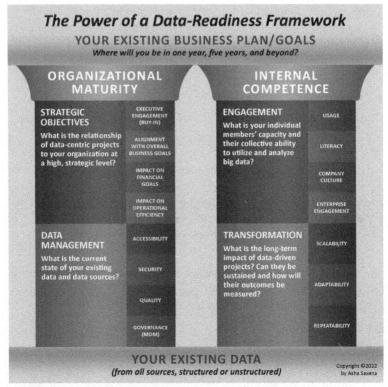

The Power of a Data-Readiness Framework

YOUR EXISTING BUSINESS PLAN/GOALS
Where will you be in one year, five years, and beyond?

ORGANIZATIONAL MATURITY		INTERNAL COMPETENCE	
STRATEGIC OBJECTIVES What is the relationship of data-centric projects to your organization at a high, strategic level?	EXECUTIVE ENGAGEMENT (BUY-IN) ALIGNMENT WITH OVERALL BUSINESS GOALS IMPACT ON FINANCIAL GOALS IMPACT ON OPERATIONAL EFFICIENCY	**ENGAGEMENT** What is your individual members' capacity and their collective ability to utilize and analyze big data?	USAGE LITERACY COMPANY CULTURE ENTERPRISE ENGAGEMENT
DATA MANAGEMENT What is the current state of your existing data and data sources?	ACCESSIBILITY SECURITY QUALITY GOVERNANCE (MDM)	**TRANSFORMATION** What is the long-term impact of data-driven projects? Can they be sustained and how will their outcomes be measured?	SCALABILITY ADAPTABILITY REPEATABILITY

YOUR EXISTING DATA
(from all sources, structured or unstructured)

Copyright ©2022
by Asha Saxena

Businesses must have both organizational maturity and internal competence in order to fully utilize their data and AI in support of established business goals.

Organizational Maturity and Strategic Objectives

Before a company can address the technical aspects of big data and AI, its leadership must adopt a different mindset. As discussed in chapter 2, many companies tend to use data only to ask, "What happened?" (also known as *descriptive* analytics) rather than, "How can we make it happen?" (or *prescriptive* analytics). The difference is important.

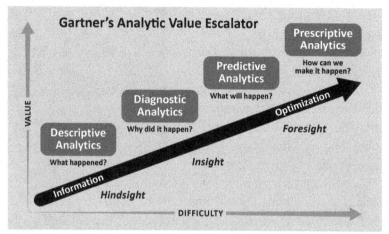

In 2013, the Gartner Group distinguished four distinct levels of big data and analytics.[7]

Such a forward-looking mindset does not happen overnight, so the best way to begin securing buy-in is by asking some basic questions:*

- *Is there executive buy-in to the long-term value of data-centric strategies?*
- *Is the data strategy aligned with overall business goals?*
- *Are data-centered projects directly related to future financial impact?*
- *Are data being used to enhance operational effectiveness?*

Executive Engagement. Technology leaders have long known the importance of executive buy-in—and how to best obtain it.[8] It includes showing how the technology supports the strategic goals and values of decision makers. But thanks to our misconceptions

---

* These are posed as "yes-no" questions. However, as I have experienced through many consulting engagements, they will inevitably lead to longer discussions and not a small amount of soul searching.

about AI and big data, executive and departmental buy-in is still the single greatest hurdle to such initiatives on a grand scale.

Buy-in means more than giving lip service, or even acknowledging the examples spelled out in part one of this book. C-level executives' buy-in must be based

STRATEGIC OBJECTIVES	EXECUTIVE ENGAGEMENT (BUY-IN)
What is the relationship of data-centric projects to your organization at a high, strategic level?	ALIGNMENT WITH OVERALL BUSINESS GOALS
	IMPACT ON FINANCIAL GOALS
	IMPACT ON OPERATIONAL EFFICIENCY

on alignment with business goals, including greater financial benefit, cost-saving operational efficiency, or both. Farsighted CEOs will also consider whether or not the company's use of data is ethical and sustainable, for that will ultimately affect their financial success. Let's consider a hypothetical example:

> The CEO of a retail bank wants to induce more members of the local community to apply for credit. The bank has ready access to an applicant's credit history and other sources of descriptive analytics, but they do not know enough about their potential customers, their buying habits, why they need credit, and the likelihood that they will use it in a positive, responsible, and sustainable way. Therefore, the bank's outreach efforts are mainly blind luck.
>
> At one point, a data specialist proposes a project, collecting and analyzing consumer data from various sources by zip code, with the goal of creating a profile or persona to whom the bank's message should be tailored.
>
> Clearly, such a project is aligned with the bank's overall goal: to attract a greater percentage of qualified credit applicants. But to get buy-in (and budget approval) from the CEO will require more. For example, the data must support the following objectives:
>
> - A verifiable predictive model that includes the projected number of qualified new applicants and their contribution to the bank's financial goals;

- A process that shortens or streamlines the credit application process for such individuals—increasing the bank's operational efficiency and lowering costs;
- A positive ROI showing the verifiable financial impact of the project;
- Safeguards against potential bias in the data that might result in withholding credit based on gender or race.

This scenario can be replicated in countless other types of business, regardless of which quadrant it occupies. Some companies will require more proof-of-concept or trial projects, of course, but so long as the use of data clearly supports these objectives, executive buy-in is likely.

Alignment. Once top-level buy-in is obtained, the next challenge is to realign the thinking of technical leadership. CTOs and IT managers are often brilliant and highly professional. They are highly unlikely to believe in popular mythology surrounding AI and big data, but their data habits may not always be conducive to disruptive new approaches.

There is often a disconnect between technology leaders within a company and the customers and employees for whom a data project is intended. Many times, tech leaders will build extensive applications, or re-engineer entire systems, while forgetting to sufficiently educate their constituents. The resulting lack of adoption usually means that the outcome will not be adequately measured or aligned with any strategic goals.

IT departments in larger companies also tend to focus on historical transactions. After all, keeping track of which products or services have sold, where they sold, how much is in inventory, and other myriad financial data, are vital aspects of modern business. But a company's IT habits can often make it difficult to use data in new ways.

Data scientist Wendy Lawhead experienced this phenomenon in her work at auto parts retailer AutoZone. "With over 4,000 stores at the time, they knew what parts sold in particular areas of the country," she said, "but they didn't know their customers' buying patterns or preferences. They didn't even have a rewards card program. So, I told the category managers, 'You don't really know what to put on the shelves unless you really know who your customer is.'" After applying clustering analysis and predictive analytics, the company began introducing products in selected stores, knowing that they would resonate with their customers. The chain now has over 6,400 stores worldwide.

Financial Goals and Efficiency. Top line financial growth or cost savings may serve as a strong incentive for a company to pursue a data-driven strategy. However, past financial transaction data alone are not sufficient. They must also be linked to customer or other constituent behavioral data. This may rely directly on data from ecommerce or customer service apps—where the customer is logged in—or on more unstructured data gathered from social media apps and websites used by typical consumers. By gauging the popularity of a particular type of product or service, the company can project the potential financial benefit.

The process of organizational maturity does not happen overnight. But once a company in any of the quadrants discussed in chapter 5 successfully undertakes a data-driven project aligned with their goals, they are more likely to embrace AI and big data on a larger scale. Whether the data is used to enhance operational efficiency (the Optimizer strategy) or to inform new product development (the Innovator strategy), the fact that a company is already doing so in one area can be the basis for doing so in others.

A striking, albeit slightly ironic example of this can be found at AI software developer RChilli. Founded in 2010, the company uses an AI framework, natural language processing, and machine learning to rapidly parse multilingual resumes and other unstructured data, automatically, to populate over 140 fields of data relevant to job recruiters.

RChilli's software's ability to efficiently automate the tedious aspects of sorting through candidates' CVs has increased recruiter efficiency by 62 percent, according to CEO Vinay Johar. It also includes mechanisms for filtering out implicit bias and has updated its parser to comply with strict European privacy requirements. As a result, RChilli software has been broadly adopted by HR departments and is used in multiple job board and ERP systems around the world.

But more recently the company also found that the business value of AI was not limited to its own product offerings.

Determining the company's marketing priorities was done initially in the traditional manner—by intuitively predicting which industries and geographic regions were most likely to adopt their resume-parsing technology. But it became obvious that there was a more accurate, data-centric way to predict and prioritize geographic regions of opportunity. "Our system processes almost 4.3 billion documents a year," Johar said. "Our log file tells us the domain and geographic information from which they come. That is enough for us to understand what is happening in the industry. Based on that intelligence, we can decide where to expand."

The company combines such information with other data sets, including public data on job market trends and customer placement success rates, with remarkable results. They know, for example, that the demand for a particular set of skills in OLED manufacturing is increasing in China or the Middle East. So then they know what companies will need more efficient recruitment tools. As a result of this process, RChilli has been able to shorten its sales cycle by 42 percent, according to Johar.

Despite obvious buy-in at the top, RChilli did not always apply a data-driven methodology to sales performance. "At one point, we would just say, 'This was our revenue, it was expensive, not very profitable, but the job is done.' That was the whole calculation," he said. But then they began setting data-centric key performance indicators (KPIs), tracking results every seven to fifteen days. Starting with simple tools like Google Sheets, the company developed a single dashboard for performance-related data.

"It was a cultural change that took almost eight months to complete," Johar said. He noted that making the data broadly available has had a "flywheel" effect, not only on sales efficiency but also on company culture itself. "As people saw how their KPIs were tracking, they began operating more like a think tank," he noted. "Seeing the numbers did not make them mad; they saw that friction was there somewhere. So, they went back to the numbers, came back, and found ways to remove that friction."

With C-level buy-in and forward-looking attitudes on data usage, a company can be well on its way to becoming a Multiplier business. But that's only part of the organizational aspect of data readiness.

Organizational Maturity and Data Management

The second, practical aspect of organizational maturity is how well it manages the actual data and their sources. Data management should always be tied to business strategy, goals, and priorities. A recent Gartner Group article pointed out that organizations too often orient data practices around the data rather than business values and outcomes.[9] This makes it difficult to have meaningful conversations with executives and other key stakeholders.

How well your company handles its data today is a foundation for applying transformational AI and big data initiatives in the future. There are many tools and organizations involved in measuring and implementing good data management, but one can begin

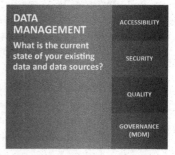

DATA MANAGEMENT

What is the current state of your existing data and data sources?

ACCESSIBILITY

SECURITY

QUALITY

GOVERNANCE (MDM)

to evaluate this aspect of organizational maturity by asking basic, preliminary questions:

- *Are your data broadly accessible across all levels of your organization?*
- *Are your data secure and safeguarded against malicious or improper use?*
- *What is the quality or trustworthiness of your data (and its descriptive metadata)?*
- *Are all your data consistently managed across all your key data sources, or are they siloed and unrelated to each other?*

●———————●

Data Accessibility has been an issue since the dawn of the digital information age and is growing exponentially ever since. Having the three v's of big data (volume, variety, and velocity) is meaningless to businesses and individual team members if they cannot access it. We've come a long way from the days of sequential access—reading data from magnetic tape—but even with near-real-time access available today, not all companies have made it easy for an individual in one department to find a relevant piece of data controlled by another department. In fact, they may not even know what to look for, much less how or why it should be used.

Artificial intelligence can offer solutions to the accessibility issue. Conversational AI, in the form of chatbots, can allow authorized users to access complex databases with simple plain language inquiries. More sophisticated AI can enable departments to have better dashboard views of all company-relevant data sets. Of course, that will require individual departments to release that information, as we'll discuss later on.

Data Security is closely tied to accessibility. Without security, there is no trust, and ultimately no buy-in from those whose data are essential for so many AI initiatives. The malicious or improper use of private data, from personal information to proprietary research, is a painful and perennial problem—one that tends to outpace the efforts of IT security departments and governments. It has necessitated ever more complex systems for maintaining authorized user access. Unfortunately, that very complexity can prevent or at least discourage users in one department from benefiting from the data of another. Data privacy legislation such as GDPR[10] is an important first step, but more is needed. GDPR holds that personal data may not be processed unless at least one out of six different conditions are met, including consent of the subject. While this begins to grant more power to individuals to protect their information, the law has proved difficult to enforce.[11] While every company can improve its own level of broad data accessibility and general security, these issues are difficult to resolve manually.

Companies may be afraid to use artificial intelligence techniques if they believe the collected data is not secure, or if AI is behind malware or ransomware attacks that hold companies hostage. While that last part is true, AI is also an extremely powerful means of detecting and blocking the malware that escapes detection by conventional antivirus software.[12]

AI is increasingly used to detect malicious attempts to read or use private or sensitive data. For example, most banks use AI to detect anomalous spending behavior that might be the result of a data breach. In most cases, the human account holders are the means by which the AI learns to better distinguish genuine transactions from fraudulent ones. As promising as this is, however, the use of AI to defend private or sensitive data must begin with a willingness to see data not as an isolated repository but as a connected piece of a much larger puzzle.

Later in the chapter, we'll explore some of the open-source tools that will make these issues easier to solve. With data access in particular, there are hopeful signs. In scientific research, there are already proposed models for making AI tools and data open source and user friendly for biomedical and healthcare domains[13] and in materials science research.[14] Other science disciplines, and eventually the general IT community, are likely to follow suit.

Data Quality is an issue that's easy to explain but hard to resolve. I'm sure you have experienced the disappointment of receiving a spreadsheet that is both filled with data and devoid of meaning. Even experienced users can make mistakes in how data are labeled and grouped, the basis for making calculations, and other data handling issues.[15] Now, take that common experience and apply it to a company's data infrastructure as a whole. When you consider the sheer volume, variety, and velocity of available data—and its importance to business growth—the prospect of erroneous or misleading data is a serious one.

Data quality has many dimensions,[16] including basic accuracy, consistency across multiple data sets, and objectivity or freedom from bias. It also has varying thresholds, depending on whether the primary interest is scientific, governmental, or commercial. In each case, the cost of poor data quality is high. According to Gartner research, the *average* financial impact of poor data quality on organizations is about $15 million every year.[17] That of course does not include the missed opportunities for exponential growth that big data and AI can afford.

There are of course common-sense steps for improving data quality. These include establishing a clear connection between data impact and KPIs and between data quality improvement and business outcomes.[18] Other steps, including designing and implementing data quality dashboards for critical assets, are widely accepted IT practices, although they typically require significant financial resources.

Improving data quality is clearly a prerequisite for effectively implementing AI and machine learning. Noted computer scientist Andrew Ng affirmed this basic tenet in his public letter on data-centric versus model-centric AI:

> *"It's a common joke that 80 percent of machine learning is actually data cleaning, as though that were a lesser task. My view is that if 80 percent of our work is data preparation, then ensuring data quality is the important work of a machine learning team."* [19]

However, AI itself can also offer solutions to data quality problems. Among other things, it can automatically identify duplicate records and detect anomalies caused by human error—as well as automate the data capture process.

The final issue related to organizational maturity is basic to data management itself, namely *master data management* or MDM. This is based on the idea that there should be a "single version of the truth" for critical business data. Ideally, this involves creating a single master record for each significant entity, item, or event, from multiple data sources and applications—to the point where the information contained in that record is a consistent data definition and a trusted source for making business decisions. [20]

In practice, however, there are often several versions of the same or comparable data, housed in separate, departmental silos and operating under very different classifications. This often occurs as the result of mergers or acquisitions where the original companies' IT departments differed significantly in their systems and practices. It's also the natural result of each department pursuing its own independent data strategy. When departmental goals and KPIs diverge, both data collection and classification typically take on different forms, resulting in unnecessary duplication and misalignment.

The relationship between MDM and AI is yet another chicken-and-egg dilemma. Consistent non-siloed data are indeed fundamental to transformational AI projects. In his 2020 *Forbes* column, Unilever's Nallan Sriraman noted that AI and machine learning predictions are only as good as their weakest link—the master data.[21] However, commenting on Sriraman's article, Zingg founder Sonal Goyal added the caveat that legacy MDM systems may not be up to the task. "With all its promise of breaking data silos," she said, "older master data technology is riddled with long configuration cycles, complex deployments as well as hard-coded rules making both addition of new data sources as well as consumption of master data by base applications cumbersome."[22]

Fortunately, as is the case with improving data quality, AI itself can be deployed to improve a company's master data management. AI and machine learning technologies are now being used to automate many MDM functions, including identifying domain types, matching/merging, data mapping, and categorizing data.[23] Both commercial and open-source tools are emerging, promising to take on trivial and recurring MDM tasks[24] and add increased precision to planning and forecasting.

Once you have addressed or begun to address the strategic alignment and data management aspects of your company's organizational maturity, you are ready to tackle the internal competence aspects of the AI data readiness framework. Like the first "column," it may sound intimidating at first, but it can be achieved readily by most businesses and nonprofits—and will result in exponential growth.

Internal Competence and Engagement

The second "column" of data readiness is about two things—your people and your tool set. Both are indispensable. Without a data-driven company culture, all the other elements described in this chapter will be useless. And without the tools to make data initiatives scalable and adaptable, companies will not have the momentum to become Multipliers.

The *people* aspect of internal competence applies both to individuals and to company culture as a whole. Executives and managers do not need to become data scientists, of course. However, their individual data usage habits and literacy are critical to building a company culture and engagement level that can take full advantage of data-centric projects. Let's start with some basic questions:

- *Are key individuals able (and willing) to view, comprehend, and utilize relevant data from across the organization?*
- *Do non-IT individuals understand the basic nature and value of data?*
- *Does the organization as a whole have a positive, reality-based attitude towards the value of data—including big data and AI?*
- *Is the organization committed to including all stakeholders, internal and external, as integral to its data strategy?*

Data Use. Most human beings need help in making sense of quantitative information. The sheer volume of data—growing exponentially as you read this—is overwhelming. To make it all meaningful requires interpretation, preferably by someone with an understanding of data science, visual design, *and* human psychology. This has been the case long before the advent of digital displays, as Yale professor Edward Tufte famously summarized in his book *The Visual Display of Quantitative Information*:

"Often the most effective way to describe, explore, and summarize a set of numbers— even a very large set—is to look at a picture of those numbers." [25]

Of course, static information displays—charts and graphs— have been superseded by dynamic digital representations, capable of change in real time as new data become available. In the business world, these displays have come to be known as data dashboards,[26] conveying a top-of-mind view of the performance and status information deemed most important to decision makers within the organization. Perhaps the most famous example is the Bloomberg Terminal,[27] first introduced in 1982. For a mere $24,000 per year, investment professionals have real-time access to global financial data, company and fund performance, news feeds, and a host of other visually represented data, on which to base their transaction decisions.

Today, web-enabled data dashboards are commonplace, and used for every imaginable type of business intelligence. In theory, the dashboard approach is ideal for facilitating projects involving big data and AI. At their most basic level, dashboards allow anyone in an organization to *view* the data—preferably in a visually meaningful context—and more significantly use the data to make business decisions that result in exponential growth.

There are of course caveats to the use of dashboards. The mere existence of a data visualization—even a dynamic one showing real-time data—does not guarantee it will be used properly, or even used at all! The human brain can process only so much information at a time, even if it is beautifully designed. Here are some cautionary points:

- **The data may be incomplete.** As we discussed earlier in the chapter, many organizations have poorly governed information, isolated in departmental silos and not connected in meaningful ways.

- *The dashboard may be prioritizing the wrong data.* Data that seems significant to an IT professional may be irrelevant to a business decision maker. Meaningful dashboard data must be in the context of *measurable* business objectives, such as KPIs and data performance indicators (DPIs), which we'll discuss in chapter 8.

- *Users may not be aware of the data's significance*, or they may not have an incentive to use it. This falls under data literacy, which we'll discuss next.

- *Most dashboards display existing or past occurrences*, but do not (or cannot) predict likely future events or prescribe a course of action. This can lead to poor business decisions, based on flawed assumptions of the data's importance, context, or causality.[28]

Despite these caveats, the dashboard approach may be the best way to facilitate the broad use of data—especially by non-technical business decision makers—in projects driven by AI. However, these dashboards must be designed to specific criteria, as outlined in a 2018 article in *Healthcare IT News*.[29] Such AI-specific dashboards must include:

- *Answers to clearly defined questions* that help users identify a prescriptive path forward.

- *KPIs that measure trends* and provide correlation to other significant data in real time.

- *A method of accountability and transparency* allowing stakeholders from multiple disciplines (finance, legal, human resources, etc.) to review the system and its underlying data, to ensure against bias and other unintended flaws.

Data Literacy. The second factor in an organization's data engagement capacity is its individual members' ability to read and understand data, to work with and analyze it, and to use data in support of a larger narrative. Unfortunately, data literacy is remarkably low today. In a 2020 Accenture report, only 25 percent of over 9,000 employees surveyed believe they are prepared to use data effectively, while only 21 percent were confident in their data literacy skills.[30]

Data literacy and technical literacy are not the same thing. As the conclusion of a report from MIT Sloan School of Management stated:

"True data literacy should enable one to think and act differently—start by understanding the real business problem and use intelligent insights to solve the right problems." [31]

The MIT Sloan report recommends that a training program should focus 80 percent of its time on data and its significance to business and only 20 percent on the technology itself. A data literacy assessment is typically used to establish a baseline of employee and management skills, while the training itself should avoid using jargon wherever possible—or at least use a vocabulary common to the organization or business division.

Above all, increasing data literacy must be based on incentives and objectives that the employee or manager finds relevant to their success—especially when it comes to big data and AI initiatives.

> IBM executive Seth Dorbin spent over ten years working on AI and big data projects designed to help IBM customers achieve major business goals. A major aspect of this work involves helping expand the data literacy of company executives—helping them understand the significance of their own data.

"For the last ten years or more, I developed what I called a 'decision portfolio,'" he said. "I sat with business leaders to determine the problems they needed to solve, and ways that AI or data can benefit them. The goal was to figure out their value of those are, their readiness to implement them, and how to prioritize them. We developed a concept we call Enterprise Design Thinking for data and AI."

Dorbin's workshop gets to the root of the problem—connecting the business strategy to building a corresponding AI strategy. Once financial value is assigned in the initial session, subsequent technical workshops with the right people are established prior to actual implementation.

"When I have conversations with people," he said, "I always point them to workshops like this, so that they can get an overarching strategy around *how* they're going to proceed in a way that's human centered and value based."

Company Culture is a broad term applied to nearly everything in business today, from inclusivity in the workplace to consultative selling. But in this case, company culture, also known as data culture,[32] refers to an organization's overall receptivity to using data—not only to describe what happened in the past but also to plan future actions and reinvent business models.

Although a robust data culture often starts with executive-level buy-in, it must also have grassroots support throughout the company. That means data-centric projects cannot be framed as "cool science experiments," or just collecting data for data's sake. Rather, they must be deployed to make good decisions—and the results of those decisions made known throughout the company. Sometimes, good old peer pressure is the way to incentivize reluctant departments to adopt a more proactive approach to data, starting with what Dorbin refers to as "quick win" projects.

"When you start, your priority should be on the parts of the business that are willing and excited to adopt," he said. "You want to get a lot of quick wins up front—so you can show how it drove value. Just as companies that use data and AI outperform those that don't, *parts* of companies that use data and AI also outperform those that don't. In executive team meetings, CEOs are going to say, 'Why aren't you doing what she's doing? She's generating more revenue cost savings with these technologies—and you're not.' That helps with the cultural shift."

Grassroots support for a data-centric company culture will increase as more people experience the benefits. However, this means unlearning old habits and misconceptions about data.

Chevron's Chief Data Officer, Ellen Nielson, described some of the issues common to businesspeople everywhere. "They believe that it's easy to have the data at hand," she said. "They're often surprised how long it takes to get the data ready. So, they can be impatient. They can't understand why it's so complicated." She suggested this might be due to an emphasis on tactical versus strategic thinking. "Sometimes, a businessperson doesn't know how to describe what really they want. They come out of a culture driven by short-term goals. They want a quick solution for one thing, and don't want to spend too much time with explaining the whole. They understand there is value but cannot describe what that value [is] or how it's measured."

Seemingly ages ago, in 2020, the *Harvard Business Review* listed ten strategic steps for companies to create a data-driven culture,[33] starting with executive buy-in (as mentioned earlier in this chapter) and ending with being transparent with one's analytical choices. The need is even more urgent today. The pandemic and the global impacts of war and disruption have made it clear that businesses and nonprofits must be even more agile than before. That can only occur in a knowledgeable, data-aware company culture.

The next building block in the data-readiness framework, **Enterprise Engagement**, is a movement[34] based on the philosophy of "stakeholder capitalism." The latter is defined as an approach that "creates returns for investors by creating value for employees, customers, supply chain and distribution partners, communities, and the environment."[35] This has proven to be much more than basic altruism. It has tangible financial rewards:

> *Companies adhering to enterprise engagement principles and belonging to the Engaged Company Stock Index (ECSI), have consistently outperformed the S&P 500 index by an average of 6.2 percent per year.*[36]

Data analytics and AI are critical components of enterprise engagement. To make decisions that provide value to *all* stakeholders—including a company's employees, partners, and customers—it must first *know* them, and have a clear understanding of their habits, their preferences, and the likelihood of their future actions. That knowledge can only be acquired and applied by understanding and leveraging big data. HR departments in particular have discovered the value of "human analytics" in turning raw data into informed decisions that ultimately improve engagement within a company.[37]

In the final analysis, businesses that combine data literacy and culture with a holistic approach to stakeholder value are far more likely to employ AI and big data initiatives that have lasting impact. They are more likely to follow the multiplier model—reinventing new business models and achieving exponential growth.

Internal Competence and Transformation

There is nothing worse for a data-centric initiative than the idea that it was a one-time success. It takes effort to gather the right data, ask the right questions, and use machine learning and/or deep learning techniques to seek relevant patterns in the data, in order to execute faster processes or actions. If all that effort has to be done all over again the next time, it will discourage or even halt future attempts. This is true even if the results are good for the organization. Big data and AI can only be transformational if the company can build on past successes with relative ease.

TRANSFORMATION

What is the long-term impact of data-driven projects? Can they be sustained and how will their outcomes be measured?

SCALABILITY

ADAPTABILITY

REPEATABILITY

The "tool set" portion of an organization's internal competence includes those technologies that will make data-centric initiatives much more than "one-off" experiments. These tools also make it clear that big data and AI are not dependent on a single person or team but can be replicated by any competent IT department or third-party service.

Scalability, **adaptability**, and **repeatability** can often be challenging when it comes to AI projects. This is often due more to the business environment than to programming difficulties. The former includes issues covered earlier in the chapter, but data professionals can offset many of these difficulties by staying focused on business outcomes. In the words of one data scientist:

"If you fail to engage the final users during the devising process of the applications, you will create a useless tool. It does not matter how good your Data Science team is, the system being created has to be driven by the business necessities. One good way to attend this is to keep the final user in touch all the way through of the experimentation and production phases.... The final solution should be constructed together with the final users." [38]

The infrastructure for creating AI and big data projects is growing more robust. In addition to expanding SaaS and cloud offerings from Amazon and other providers, a host of smaller developers are providing AI-based technologies and integration services—for a price.

But hired guns are not the only choice. Companies and their IT departments can also avail themselves of a wide array of non-proprietary resources. This includes **open-source AI code** from GitHub and other exchanges. These charge modest annual subscription fees but offer sizeable development savings by allowing data analysts to freely copy, modify, and build upon others' work. True to the open-source model, AI and machine learning developers often share their work on such exchanges, building up a "critical mass" of practical data analytics tools.

The open-source approach to AI has additional benefits. It has accelerated AI adoption, promoting healthy competition and frequently resulting in "accessible, robust, and high-quality code," according to a Brookings Institution report.[39] It has also helped reduce AI bias by giving scientists more time and resources to develop transparent, explainable data models. "For those engaged, but busy, data scientists, open-source code can be incredibly helpful in discovering and mitigating discriminatory aspects of machine learning," the report concluded.

Conclusions

Every business or nonprofit has the potential to collect the data needed to fuel meaningful AI projects. Whether or not that business is limited in its growth and innovation potential, it has the ability to change its cultural and technical readiness to embrace data-centric approaches to problem solving—and ultimately become a multiplier business.

In the next chapter, we will explore the specific question of *how* to accomplish this audacious-sounding goal.

Prioritizing the Power Zone

Octothorpe management was considering several different growth strategies, each of which potentially could be guided by data and AI initiatives. The question was, which project should be tackled first? Nontraditional catering situations and impromptu "pop-up" food services were emerging. At the same time, their traditional customer base of restaurants was looking to set up franchise locations. Each of these trends represented growth potential for delivering specialty food products, but without the data, expanding their operations would rely on guesswork.

The company knew it would be foolish to pursue multiple projects at once, so they evaluated the available data set for each of several projects. Their store of information from existing customers—what they ordered, how well or how poorly the delivery went, and so on—was by far the most relevant and compelling data. Then they rated the business value of using that data. Specifically, they predicted that, if used to guide marketing content aimed at restaurants and caterers nationwide, the data would fuel new customer acquisition and increased sales.

By doing this, Octothorpe defined the priority "power zone" for a data-driven campaign—in this case to improve their marketing efforts with meaningful and measurable goals. Chapter 7 is a blueprint for setting such priorities, first by rating the quality of the available data, and second by rating a project's business value in terms that can be measured—both during and after the project's run.

CHAPTER 7

Becoming a Multiplier

Now we're at the third and most important step in using AI and big data. You have assessed the current state of your organization and taken stock of its data readiness. The third step is to **prioritize the one area that would yield the most value** by applying AI and data solutions. By doing so, you will have begun the process of growing your business or nonprofit exponentially.

Don't despair if your business position and data readiness are not exactly where you might wish. As you will see, it is possible to define a single project that will yield good results, even within a company that is less than perfect, data-wise or in terms of potential growth. But finding a priority that will yield the best results involves something I call the "power zone," a Venn diagram of easily explored factors:

Once you have identified areas where these factors overlap, you may be tempted to apply big data and AI technologies to several projects at once. But it's not wise to go beyond one or two—especially on the first attempt. Once you've succeeded at

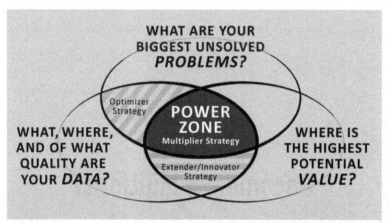

The overlap of persistent problems, rich relevant data, and potential business value is where AI and big data can have the greatest impact. A multiplier strategy is all about the speed at which you can scale data solutions based on all three elements.

obtaining measurable results, as we'll explore in chapter 8, you may want to expand your portfolio, but for now, less is definitely more. By demonstrating your first notable success in the power zone, you will draw others' attention to the potential of data to multiply business performance.

Planning a Data Strategy

In chapter 5, we touched briefly on the business model canvas approach to strategy mapping. Having an at-a-glance overview of a company's goals and means is a powerful tool for business in general, but it is also indispensable when planning an individual data project. Such a canvas is shown here:

The purpose of a Data Power Canvas is to be a comprehensive starting point for discussion by both business and data leadership. The left-to-right order is not as important as what goes in the individual spaces. The most pressing business problem may

The Data Power Canvas

Data	Problem	Data Performance	Product
	Market		Customer
	Delivery		Price/Cost

Copyright ©2022 by Asha Saxena

Defining the parameters of any data-centric project can set realistic expectations for its potential measurable impact—and prepare for solving future problems.

be known intuitively before the data are available to fully define it. In other cases, the data may be known first, as shown here, revealing the nature and scope of the problem, thus confirming the leaders' intuition.

Identifying the Most Urgent Problems

All organizations struggle with vexing problems of every kind, of course. The very nature of business—and of life—assumes that there will be *barriers* to efficiency, to profitability, or to higher aspirations. So, the first question that must be applied when identifying the *biggest* unsolved problem is:

If it remains unsolved, what exactly does this problem cost us, in terms of measurable lost efficiency, missed opportunity, or other, less tangible factors?

Not all problems have an obvious or effective AI or big data solution. But for the purposes of this chapter—and of the entire book—the ability to prioritize problems that *do* have a data-centric solution comes from a combination of sources:

- The informed **intuition** or "gut" instincts of experienced leaders on the problem's severity and cost, and
- Existing internal **data** indicating the exact nature of the problem.

There is little empirical research on the use of intuition by managers. The simple reason for this is that intuition is something taking place in the minds of individuals, not accessible to researchers. However, there's a growing body of work supporting the view that intuition is a valid psychological phenomenon—one that eventually will be recognized "as a central and necessary component of managers' decision-making tool kits."[1]

These days, it's popular to tout the power of our intuition, in a business context or otherwise. Malcolm Gladwell's 2005 bestseller, *Blink*, has many examples of how our unconscious mind can lead us to surprising and often powerful results. This happens through a process called "thin slicing"—where our unconscious mind detects patterns based on narrow slices of experience.[2] He also points out examples of how our unconscious intuitive responses can lead us to make poor choices, such as the 1920 election of President Warren Harding—a man who seemed "presidential" in the public imagination but proved to be anything but. Psychologist Daniel Kahneman further warned that our automatic unconscious thought processes, known as "System 1," are subject to many cognitive errors and biases. These result in poor decisions if we fail to "slow down and ask for reinforcement from System 2"—our more deliberate, effortful mental processes.[3]

With those caveats in mind, intuition can often be the factor in making business decisions—when the data alone are insufficient to justify choices or identify specific problems. In fact, it is often a *combination* of data and intuition that provides the necessary insight.[4]

The combination of insight and data is even more important when it comes to AI and analytics in general. As Babson College professor Thomas Davenport pointed out, "a hypothesis is an intuition about what's going on in the data you have about the world. The difference with analytics, of course, is that you don't stop with the intuition—you test the hypothesis to learn whether your intuition is correct."[5]

Davenport also noted that intuition is often the *initial* basis for analytics initiatives since few companies take the trouble of doing the actual analytical studies to find such opportunities. Gary Loveman, the CEO of Caesars (then Harrah's) casinos, intuitively believed in the "service profit chain" model—the theory that improved customer service improves financial results. Although he did not have casino-specific data at the time, his intuition fueled years of analytics projects—each with a specific ROI requirement. Starting with data from the casino's "Total Gold" members' program, the company developed a detailed understanding of customer behavior and preferences, which in turn fueled business decisions that dramatically increased customer loyalty and yielded a 14 percent gain in revenues.[6]

Intuition is also essential when the problem goes beyond the reach of traditional data analytics and requires a true AI or ML solution. Not all business problems are amenable to ML, but when they are, the final step must always be asking questions—to determine if the proposed ML processes, however brilliant technically, make sense from a rational business perspective.[7]

The other part of the problem-finding process is to look at the data you already have. Later on in the chapter, we'll discuss the different sources and types of data, and how to evaluate their relevance and value, but for now we'll consider *existing* data as signals of pressing business problems.

Deliberately or otherwise, most companies have already collected a trove of existing, internal data that, if viewed correctly, can flag business problems, and can often indicate their financial impact. Such sources include:

INTERNAL DATA SOURCE	TYPE OF DATA[8]
Call center records from customer service or technical support—text threads, recordings, and surveys	Why customers leave or stay Behavioral data
Sales, installation, or incident reports by salespeople, customer service representatives, or by field service agents or trainers	Why customers leave or stay Basic demographic data Transaction history
Marketing funnel data from CRM (customer relationship management), search, and content management systems	Referral sources Content performance
Ecommerce records recording historical customer choices and preferences	Transaction history Behavioral data
Social media data related to a company, its products, and its customers	Referral sources Content performance Behavioral data

Any one of these sources is an excellent, objective starting point for identifying problems with a potential AI or big data solution. Call center records are a particularly rich potential source for detecting costly problems. These can be relatively simple, involving metrics such as customer satisfaction and first-call resolution.[9] Such data are highly structured in nature, so conventional analytics may be sufficient to identify problems and even provide solutions. However, other call center data, especially voice recordings, are unstructured, so a more rigorous, statistical data analysis may be needed.[10]

This is an area where AI and machine learning will play an important part in detecting problems. An early study in France explored ways to identify human emotion from call center recordings.[11] This has since been used to detect high levels of stress or frustration,[12] helping call centers be more responsive and transferring calls from automated systems to human operators more effectively.

No matter what source is used in detecting a problem, the data can be used to confirm or challenge the business leader's intuitive "gut" feeling about the problem, regardless of its financial cost. Once a pressing problem has been identified, however, the next steps in the process are critical.

Existing Conditions Matter

Once you have identified your most pressing problem, it is vital to understand current business conditions—the *context* in which the problem exists. Netflix and Starbucks did not initiate their successful data strategies with a clean slate, nor did smaller companies like Coda Coffee. Like them, you must recognize and quantify the circumstances that may help or hinder your data-centric initiatives.

External *global market conditions*[13] like inflation, interest, taxes, and employment rates are of course outside the control of individual companies, but their current status and trends can have a great impact on the success or failure data-driven projects. Still less under our control are changes in governmental policy, consumer behavior, and tech disruptions. In fact, industry leaders and experts have been embarrassingly wrong about the latter, such as the 2006 *New York Times* prediction that Apple would never come out with a cell phone.[14] That's all the more reason to have a data-centric approach to understanding business and market conditions. When used well, data can always help find patterns in behavior. AI can leverage data to find trends that can be used effectively in multiple applications—to create a multiplier effect. Accessing the data related to external conditions is not as formidable as it may seem. Public data sources, as described below, are readily available on nearly all such matters. Companies do not need to update or curate such data, of course, but each public data source deemed relevant to your business *must be evaluated for its relevance and quality*. AI can then be applied to detect anomalies within potentially unreliable data sources.[15]

However, no matter how interesting global factors may be, **internal conditions** within your business, such as current distribution channels or revenue streams, are more important. They may not be the main problem your data project is intended to solve, but they are always interrelated to some degree. When Netflix and Starbucks sought to "know their customers better than they knew themselves," they already had well-established ordering and delivery channels—for DVDs and coffee products, respectively—and mountains of related data. The problem was not to make those channels work better; it was to predict what their customers wanted, regardless of the channel they used—and even if it meant adopting entirely new channels. Knowing those internal conditions was important, but not central to the problem that AI and big data needed to solve.

Finding the Right Data—and Its Relevance

When going through your existing sources of internal data sets, you may well discover that they are incomplete or you have not sufficiently managed the data as a valuable, unified resource, as discussed in the previous chapter. This should not stop you from prioritizing an area that would benefit from AI and big data, although it may limit your choices at first. (Of course, it should also incentivize you to improve your overall data readiness.)

In addition to the many often untapped sources of internal data, you can also benefit from external sources, including free public data. Tableau Software lists multiple free data sources on a wide range of topics,[16] as does G2's LearnHub[17] and Google Public Data Explorer.[18] Paid external data sources can also be obtained from companies like Dun & Bradstreet. In other words, the problem is not that there is not enough data but that we often don't know how to assess the data's value.

Before we discuss the business value of a project, we must first examine the data we intend to use and assign what I call a **Data Value Indicator** (DVI) rating. This is about much more than data *volume* or *quality*—namely, non-siloed and consistently governed across the enterprise, as outlined in the previous chapter. What I mean is that, unless the data are **clearly related to the project's intended purpose**, they will not produce the desired results.

A project team's goal for a particular project is to assign a numeric DVI rating to the chosen data set. (We will use this number later in the chapter.) This numeric assignment is not an arbitrary or a purely intuitive choice, although a team will get better at this

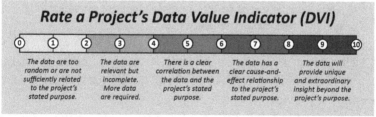

Rate a Project's Data Value Indicator (DVI)

⓪	①	②	③	④	⑤	⑥	⑦	⑧	⑨	⑩
The data are too random or are not sufficiently related to the project's stated purpose.		The data are relevant but incomplete. More data are required.		There is a clear correlation between the data and the project's stated purpose.		The data has a clear cause-and-effect relationship to the project's stated purpose.		The data will provide unique and extraordinary insight beyond the project's purpose.		

All data are not created equal! When considering the value of one's data for a particular project, always determine to what extent the use of the data will most likely achieve a desired outcome. By asking hard questions, you will be able to rate its Data Value Indicator numerically, which will be used later in the chapter to determine a project's priority.

process with experience. Assigning a high data value means that your current data set poses **meaningful questions** about actual problems. These can include measurable market conditions or trends, customer behavior, delivery issues—anything that would either help or hinder your primary business objective. For example, one can theorize that more customers would prefer to order such-and-such product on their smartphones, but unless the data can prove that assumption, the project's DVI will be low.

These questions are not about business issues such as greater efficiency or revenue, which are covered in the next section. Rather they are about the data's *relevance*. For example, "If we analyze this particular data set, will we know if consumers prefer red or green apples?" or "Will we know what time of day is best for stockholder meetings?" or "Will we find the best people and location for a new office" or "Will we find out something we hadn't even considered before?" The questions can be related to any aspect of the problem, including the possibility of unforeseen outcomes, but they must have a solid foundation:

- Questions about the data and their value must be meaningful in the real world.
- Answers to questions must provide actual knowledge about the most pressing issues facing a business or nonprofit.
- They must be based on the competence and confidence of IT and business leadership alike.

The project must have a purpose—to solve a known problem or uncover a new opportunity. Therefore, the data set and the answers it provides via basic analytics, AI, or machine learning must also support that purpose. If those answers only suggest a correlation between the two, then the DV should only be around five, but if there's a direct and logical cause-and-effect relationship, the DV should be around seven.

This exercise will become more efficient over time, especially if a business or nonprofit has taken the data-readiness steps in chapter 6 seriously. Once a fair number of successful data projects have been completed, you will be more confident in assigning an even higher DVI of eight or nine, with reasonable expectations that the data will provide unique insights and lead you to pursue a multiplier strategy. Then, the next stage is to evaluate its business value.

The Business Value of Data

By now, you probably already agree that collecting and using data for its own sake—or as a "cool science project"—is a self-defeating mindset. By contrast, pursuing a more business-oriented approach will help undo stereotypes about IT professionals as insular or controlling. As author and tech investor Romi Mahajan put it, "When told that they are too far removed from the business, IT pros ought to remind everyone that in modern organizations, the business and IT departments are converging and that the latter enables the former."[19]

To be successful, every data project must have a clearly defined **Business Value Indicator** (BVI) for which a numeric value may be assigned:

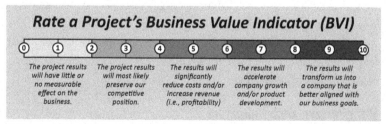

Rate a Project's Business Value Indicator (BVI)

| 0 | 1 | 2 | 3 | 4 | 5 | 6 | 7 | 8 | 9 | 10 |

| The project results will have little or no measurable effect on the business. | The project results will most likely preserve our competitive position. | The results will significantly reduce costs and/or increase revenue (i.e., profitability) | The results will accelerate company growth and/or product development. | The results will transform us into a company that is better aligned with our business goals. |

Data-centric projects always have a relative value to the success of a business. Rating that value numerically may start with an intuitive hypothesis by both business and IT leaders but must always include tangible measurable results.

Above all, a project's business value must be *measurable*. No matter how interesting an AI or ML project may seem, if its results cannot be quantitatively measured, then it cannot be considered valuable to the health or growth of the business. For example, "brand loyalty" is one of the aspirational goals of every marketing campaign on the planet. But unless the proposed data project actually measures how consumers *feel* about the brand, it is speculative at best. In the past, such measurements could only be obtained through costly surveys and focus groups but now can also be gathered via AI.

In chapter 8, we will be discussing the all-important step of measuring the results of any data-centric project—and what that means when it comes to scaling such projects to achieve even higher goals. However, in order to measure anything, one must first define the parameters of those measurable results. In other words, what do we expect to see proven—or disproven—at the end of the day?

Some of these results will be relatively easy to discover, such as those related to reducing costs or increasing revenue. In this model, such potential results would yield a BVI rating of around five. Other potential results, such as increased company growth or new product development—deserving in a BVI rating of seven or so—must be measured over a longer period of time. In every case, however, assigning a rating must be done realistically, balancing the hard requirements of quantitative measurement with the more aspirational qualitative measurements that non-IT professionals tend to prefer.

Data Performance Indicators

Once you have rated the relevance of a project's data and its value to the business, you can calculate something I refer to as its Data Performance Index, or DPI. It is here that the potential power of

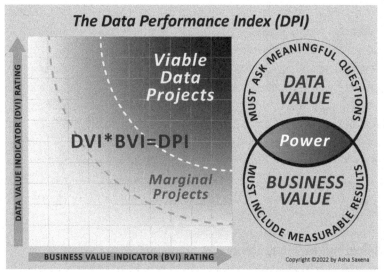

The Data Performance Index (DPI)

Viable Data Projects

DVI*BVI=DPI

Marginal Projects

DATA VALUE
MUST ASK MEANINGFUL QUESTIONS

Power

BUSINESS VALUE
MUST INCLUDE MEASURABLE RESULTS

DATA VALUE INDICATOR (DVI) RATING

BUSINESS VALUE INDICATOR (BVI) RATING

Copyright ©2022 by Asha Saxena

The higher a project's Data Performance Index (DPI), the more likely it is to produce exponential results. Viable data projects must have a high data value, a high business value, or both. Once a project's DPI has been assigned as the basis for moving forward, the validity of its underlying questions (DVI) and the success of its results (BVI) must be continuously evaluated and compared with our original rating.

AI and big data can be quantified, allowing us to predict, with high confidence, that a data project can transform a business.

This number, like its antecedents, is not an arbitrary one. It is based on real-world evaluations of a data set's intrinsic value, relevance, and business impact. It not only indicates a project's priority relative to other data projects, but it also provides an objective basis for measuring its success—which will be discussed in greater detail in the next chapter.

Under this model, the project with the highest combination of data and business value should be given the highest priority. For example, if service call data could prove a strong correlation with repeat business, its DVI would be rated at six. Then, if repeat business represented a significant top line growth potential (a desirable and highly measurable goal), its DVI could be rated at seven. The resulting DPI of forty-two would justify making it a priority over a lesser project.

The DPI rating not only will help a company prioritize a project, but also will help determine how much to invest in it. For example, a customer service improvement project may have a very high, measurable BVI but the existing data set may be too meager to justify a full-on AI or machine learning approach. The lower DPI rating would then warrant a simpler, more traditional approach.

Selecting the Right Approach

Once a problem and its data set are well defined, and a measurable performance standard assigned, the next step in completing the data power canvas is to determine which method to adopt in solving it. This may involve predictive analytics or something more autonomous, namely AI or ML where the algorithms can improve themselves over time. While these approaches are interrelated, they have important differences.[20]

The choice of which method to use is based on several factors. These include not only cost (which is changing almost daily) but also the company's state of data readiness and the quality (or DVI) of the actual data set being used for the project.

As discussed earlier, traditional data analytics can be merely descriptive or diagnostic—answering the questions, "What happened, and why?" However, they can also be predictive and even prescriptive—helping companies understand what is likely to happen and what might be done about it.

What distinguishes "ordinary" analytics from its AI counterpart is that the former is static and driven by human hypothesis.[21] While it can have significant value in solving business problems, traditional analytics requires a knowledgeable human—or a team of them—not only to visualize the problem but also to interpret the results subjectively and point out the most beneficial response.

That is not to say that analytics should be avoided. Far from it. For lower DPI projects, an analytics approach is ideal, provided it is within the scope of human testing and interpretation. Well-designed data dashboards will always have a place, provided those who use them understand their limitations. However, if the data set in question is too large and complex to be managed and interpreted by humans alone, then either artificial intelligence or machine learning (which are *not* synonymous[22]) are the preferred methods to use. Compared with analytics alone, both AI and ML are dynamic, autonomous, and driven by whatever the data are—regardless of the human hypothesis. In fact, an AI approach can more easily disprove a faulty hypothesis and improve upon the company's data strategy.

At this point in the data power canvas, be sure to include all the tools and proposed parameters for the analytics or AI method. By doing so, you can then proceed to the intended goal for the project.

Establishing the Goal

The final task (other than measuring and scaling the results, which will be covered in chapter 8) is to set the project's goals. These can be about relatively incremental improvements, effecting things like prices, costs, or distribution channels. They can also be about enlarging the business, acquiring new customers, or guiding the development of new products, as outlined in chapter 5. However, goals should also include the possibility of significantly reinventing your business model, even to the point of discarding previous models.

The goals listed on a data power canvas should be as explicit as possible, with two important caveats:

- *The data may prove OR disprove your assumptions.* Both outcomes are valuable. The successful result of a data-driven project or initiative may be not only to lead you into exponential growth but also to protect your company from making disastrous choices.

- *Always expect the unexpected.* Artificial intelligence and machine learning have the potential to encompass far more data—structured and unstructured—than any team of IT experts could ever handle on their own. So, one must be prepared to find unforeseen or unexpected conclusions. By definition, AI is something designed not only to make light of routine tasks, such as sifting through oceans of data, but also to simulate human decision making. While AI may never become sentient in the Hollywood sense, it can certainly arrive at conclusions and suggest courses of action that we haven't thought of.

By prioritizing and quantifying a data project in this manner—at the "power intersection" of your greatest business challenge, your data, and its potential value—you will create the opportunity for the AI Factor to produce exponential growth.

In the next chapter, we'll explore the execution of such a strategy, including ways to measure the results, adapt and scale them to other projects, and transform your business accordingly.

All Systems Go

Having decided on a course of action, Octothorpe found a suitable partner: an agency well versed in data and AI solutions. Open-source AI tools were used to extract significant customer preferences from the ever-growing store of customer feedback. This guided the creation of marketing content tailored to the many different available advertising and social media channels.

To maintain the necessary volume of marketing content, the agency used open-source NLP to generate rough copy, which was monitored and edited by human writers. It also applied extensive A/B testing and other rigorous protocols—not only to gauge the effectiveness of different content under different conditions but also to prioritize ad spending in channels where it would be most effective.

Throughout the campaign, the team measured not only the usual advertising metrics (open rates, click-throughs, and the like) but also the progress of clients through the marketing funnel, correlated with the content viewed. In the end, they experienced a significant increase in conversion and retention, with an increase in revenue that more than justified the cost of the project.

Beyond that, the team's success also inspired follow-up projects related to more efficient delivery processes. Data generated from the project has also revealed new customer opportunities beyond restaurants and caterers for which the same data and AI methods may be applied.

Octothorpe's successful implementation, measurement, and potential for scaling is an example of the methods described in chapter 8. If a data project measurably lives up to its prescribed data and business potential, then its positive impact will not be limited to that project alone. By utilizing the experience, tools, skill sets, and even the resulting data from a single, well-designed project, a company can expand to even greater goals—increasing their value exponentially.

CHAPTER 8

Implementing, Measuring, and Scaling the AI Factor

So far, we have discussed the essential steps involved in *planning* a viable data and AI strategy. Once you have assessed the inherent nature of your business or nonprofit (the four quadrants), its data readiness, and mapped and prioritized a data project (based on its value), then comes the fun part—making it happen and optimizing the results.

Having the right data team is essential to implementing the AI Factor. A good team will help you build momentum, especially when the initial projects are designed to produce quick wins. For many smaller companies, the team will likely include external partners or consultants with the necessary knowledge and experience. This is especially true when seeking specialized help in a particular business discipline, such as digital marketing, recruitment and hiring, product support, supply chain efficiency, or R&D. But no matter how the team is retained, it must include key members with defined roles.

Building the right data team is no small matter.[1] Not everyone on the team needs to be a "data scientist," of course, but each role is essential. They include:

- **An executive sponsor** or advocate—as discussed earlier in chapter 6;
- **A data engineer**—one who defines and implements data into the overall AI architecture;
- **A data scientist**—one who is qualified to explore data to extract actionable information;
- **A development operations engineer** (or DevOps)—one who ensures that the solutions are rolled out and managed;
- **A business analyst**—one who acts as a translator of sorts, both to assess the needs that a data project should meet and to convey the results on which decisions are made.

In many larger, more traditional companies, analytics initiatives tend to be centralized, with a single data team serving an entire organization. Other organizations lean towards a decentralized or hybrid approach, where each business unit or department has its own data resources, processes, and teams. Neither approach is inherently wrong, but the size and composition of one's data team(s) should be determined by the organization's overall data strategy.[2] Regardless of the structural approach, however, communication is essential.

> "Hire good people with strong communication skills and everything else becomes a lot easier," according to Greg Waldman, Senior Director of Business Intelligence at Toast. "Good people will lead you to other great people, and you can hire the smartest people in the world, but if they can't communicate their analyses to less technical folks, they simply won't be successful."[3]

The criteria for selecting the right data team are the same, whether you are retaining a consultancy or hiring your own people:

- **Experience with data models and approaches** that are not limited to traditional structured data and isolated or siloed data repositories. In other words, they must understand and be prepared to follow the data-readiness process described in chapter 6.

- **A focus on business objectives first** when it comes to data and AI. Every project must have a sufficiently high and measurable DPI. That is, it must have a highly rated Business Value Indicator (BVI) and a comparably high Data Value Indicator (DVI), as discussed in chapter 7.

This chapter will show how data projects can be executed and measured—with the help of an outside consultancy or on one's own. However, when it comes to achieving exponential growth, they all follow the same basic principles. If a project's measured performance matches or exceeds that of its predicted business value, then it will be the cause of real business growth. It will also become a reliable template for future projects.

The first step in executing a data project is **to confirm the existing data's value and relevance to the main business objective**. For example, in a recruitment and hiring initiative, the primary data are typically contained in resumes and online job board submissions. Much of the data will be unstructured, of course, written by candidates trying to influence human readers. As we discussed in the previous chapter, it would be reasonable to presume that such data are highly relevant, and thus deserve to be rated highly (DVI). The problem of course is that there are so many resumés and so little time to review them properly. Fortunately, as developer RChilli demonstrated,[4] unstructured data from resumés and other sources can be used to populate meaningful data fields using an AI parser software. Such data are measured as to a candidate's fitness for specific jobs, and then used to accurately identify the ideal candidates—all while filtering out undue bias.

If the initial data set is relevant to the business objective, the next step is **to create a means of collecting more data** of the same kind. Ideally, this additional data should be amenable to a machine learning process, whereby the accuracy of AI decisions may be refined and improved. In the above example, resumés in Word or other formats can be supplemented by online job submission forms and subsequent correspondence with candidates and even public posts on social media, all overseen by recruiting agencies or HR departments. Feedback from those human sources, confirming or modifying the AI's job matching decision, is a reliable means of not only expanding the data but also improving AI choices.

Keep in mind that the initial data set does not have to be enormous in order to build a reliable AI model, as Stanford professor Andrew Ng noted in 2019:[5]

> "You can create value even without having 'big data,' which is often overhyped. Some businesses, such as web search, have a long tail of queries, and so search engines with more data do perform better. However, not all businesses have this amount of data, and it may be possible to build a valuable AI system with perhaps as few as 100–1000 data records (though more does not hurt). *Do not choose projects just because you have a lot of data in industry X and believe the AI team will figure out how to turn this data into value* (emphasis added). Projects like this tend to fail. It is important to develop a thesis upfront about how specifically an AI system will create value."

The final implementation step is **to set up a reliable means of measuring the results**. In chapter 7, we discussed assigning a business value to a data project by asking questions related to real business issues. If the questions or goals are objective in nature (such as reduced time spent searching for qualified job candidates in the above example), then measurement will be straightforward. Other more nuanced questions might well be appropriate, but measuring whether or not those goals have been met should be done with care.

As we described in the previous chapter, determining the priority of a data project is done by multiplying the assigned Data Value Indicator (DVI) by the assigned Business Value Indicator (BVI) to come up with a numeric score—the Data Performance Index (DPI). This leads us to a simple, perhaps simplistic formula for judging the success of a project using data and AI, namely:

To be considered successful, a project's measured DPI must be equal to or greater than its projected DPI.

The value and relevance of the data may be intuitively presumed, as can the value of the project from a business perspective. But until those presumptions are borne out with authentic measured results, then the project is merely an exercise.

Guarding Against Assumptions

When measuring the results of a data-centric project, there is always a danger that we will be unduly influenced by our own human cognitive errors. As psychologist Daniel Kahneman so ably pointed out,[6] we are all prone to draw conclusions based not on conscious logical reasoning but on unconscious bias. This affects well-meaning business and technology leaders alike, for the simple reason that both are quite human. When it comes to data-centric projects, these potential errors include:

Confusing Correlation with Causation. A positive business result is always welcome news, but when it occurs within the same timeframe as a data-centric project, the temptation will always be to draw a direct cause-and-effect line between the two. The fact is that, in many cases involving data, correlation and causation have nothing to do with one another. This is especially true when using *visual* representations of the data, in dynamic dashboards or in summary reports. Humans are prone to see patterns in the world around them—even when such patterns have no real meaning. If two data points or trend lines are visually similar, there are five possible explanations, including the possibility that the similarity is a coincidence.[7]

This does not mean correlation—visual or otherwise—should be ignored. Rather, it should be taken with a grain of salt, and explored for the *possibility* of a cause-and-effect relationship. Edward Tufte summarized the relationship well: "Empirically observed covariation (correlation) is necessary but not a sufficient condition for causality," he noted. *"Correlation is not causation, but it sure is a hint* [emphasis added]."[8]

Always be conscious of other factors that may have contributed to the result and weigh all factors—including the data-driven ones—with due consideration. The good news is that AI solutions capable of self-adjustment are more likely to identify cause-and-effect relationships accurately. In a complex world, unrelated or unanticipated causes can never be completely ruled out.

Confirmation Bias. Kahneman and others have described the age-old logical fallacy of looking for or preferring evidence that supports your pre-existing beliefs or positions. Seasoned business and technology leaders are well aware of this problem, and many take pains to avoid it. Nevertheless, because we are all too human, it remains a problem when measuring the results of data-driven projects.

Published studies have shown that confirmation bias has a lot to do with the *weighting* of evidence. In one study, "[p]artic-ipants tended to agree on the interpretation of evidence (i.e., whose hypothesis was supported by the evidence) but tended to disagree on the importance of the evidence—giving more weight to the evidence that supported their preferred hypothesis and less weight to evidence that disconfirmed it."[9] The same study also noted that the procedure known as "analysis of competing hypothesis" significantly reduced bias for participants without intelligence analysis experience.

This particular bias is not limited to business leaders hoping for positive results. It also affects their technology leader coun-terparts. While the nature of data is by definition objective, data science is a human endeavor requiring human intervention and subjective interpretation. Confirmation bias can be mitigated, however, if the original data sets and their results are analyzed by two or more data scientists, independently of one another. Other precautions may include routinely exploring contradictory hypotheses and, importantly, incorporating greater diversity in one's data science teams.[10]

For business leaders engaged in AI projects, there are also basic guidelines for recognizing and avoiding confirmation bias.11 These include the "only good news" phenomenon. Always be sus-picious if the measurements do not contain a mix of positive and negative results. Be equally suspicious if the reported metrics are limited or obscure. (Remember that the definition of *ethical* AI,[12] explored in chapter 4, includes *transparency*—namely, that an AI system must provide satisfactory explanations auditable by a competent human authority.)

Other Cognitive Errors. When measuring the results of a particular project, these and other normal cognitive biases, like framing and sunk-cost fallacies, can be mitigated by a combina-tion of factors. One is by establishing a peer review environment of sorts, allowing others to challenge basic assumptions and the significance of the data. Another is to establish ground rules in advance—parameters for what can and cannot be claimed with the data.

The most important bulwark against cognitive errors and biases, however, is the creation of a healthy, mission-focused company culture. As described in chapter 3, Domino's Pizza decided that data revealing failure and flaws were just as valuable as data indicating the potential for success. A healthy business culture cannot be based on false optimism or the fear of failure—two of the major drivers of cognitive error. Effective AI projects must allow the data to drive the hypothesis, not the other way around.

Criteria for Measurement and Action

When measuring the results of an AI or analytics project there are two separate but interrelated criteria to consider. One is purely technical. Artificial intelligence and machine learning are most effective when processing very large data sets. They also are very resource-intensive—and potentially costly—when it comes to processing capacity and speed. Fortunately, there are emerging performance benchmarks that can help quantity and measure these systems.[13] One of these, MLPerf, has shown great promise in early studies[14] and will make it easier for data professionals to gauge ML technical efficiency.

All this points to the need for faster, more scalable, power-efficient, and affordable hardware and software. In 2019, AI/ML pioneer Andrew Ng noted, "AI is transforming multiple industries, but for it to reach its full potential, we still need faster hardware and software."[15] The traditional, "big iron" approach may well prove beyond the means of most companies. But fortunately, cloud computing offers a more affordable path to the required computing power, allowing smaller companies to "punch above their weight."[16]

Accuracy in well-run AI and ML projects is typically high. However, accuracy requirements vary by situation. For hospitals, airlines, and automotive applications (think self-driving cars), AI and ML models must be scrupulously accurate—and continuously improved with human oversight. But for areas where the impact is different, such as customer service, sales and marketing, and even new product development, strict accuracy is less urgent.

Over-focusing on an AI project's accuracy may be counterproductive if steps are not taken to make sure it is also transparent and scalable.[17] The "accuracy fallacy" can distract from other factors, such as human performance factors and, of course, overall business value. According to Gramener co-founder Ganes Kesari, "even a 'wrong' model can transform your business."[18]

In addition, accuracy is not a single metric. It is one of four useful but not always easily explained statistical measures, including how to deal with false positives. As with everything else involving data science, these numbers must be evaluated in a business context, and not oversimplified to justify a prior opinion.[19]

The non-technical measurement criteria for AI projects are of course the business results. If the project's data performance index or DPI (the assigned value of the data times its assigned business value) is explicitly assigned beforehand, then there is a simple standard to be met. But to judge the results in greater detail, we must return to the data canvas model introduced in chapter 7:

Product Development

There are three areas where the results of a data project can be measured. One is the development of a new or modified product or service. PricewaterhouseCoopers found that companies using AI and ML for new product development—designated as "digital

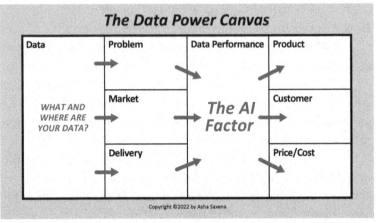

The Data Power Canvas

Data	Problem	Data Performance	Product
WHAT AND WHERE ARE YOUR DATA?	Market	The AI Factor	Customer
	Delivery		Price/Cost

Copyright ©2022 by Asha Saxena

Assuming the data are sufficient and relevant and the potential business value is adequately identified, the power of a successful AI/ML project will result in substantial, even revolutionary changes affecting product offerings, customer growth, or cost-effectiveness.

champions"—are significantly ahead in generating revenue from new products and services.[20] This applies to multiple areas of product development,[21] including:

- **Concept and specification**, where process simulation and social listening play a significant role,
- **Design and development**, including an effective combination of data analytics, AI, and Agile processes, and
- **Testing and go-to-market**, where data analytics and AI have proven to be the most effective tools.

Major technology players, including Microsoft,[22] Oracle,[23] and many others have helped other companies (and themselves) by creating AI labs to experiment with high-impact projects and develop their AI capabilities. Many of these labs also provide a data marketplace for making the models and data sets available for re-use. AI research labs also deal with the AI talent shortage by recruiting and training additional people in high-demand sectors such as biotechnology.[24]

The process begins with customer preference/experience data (positive or negative) that identifies either a potential opportunity or a flaw preventing wider adoption. Once the new product or service is released, changes in revenue are only one measurement of its success or failure. Customer feedback and especially related item purchases—driven by AI recommendation engines—provide additional data to guide product development or, should the underlying premise be proven faulty, to change direction entirely.

Such feedback need not be limited to new data following a product's release. During development, the same process—relying on known customer preference patterns—can be used to test assumptions and adjust what the product or service should be. The advantage of using AI and ML to manage this process is that, if properly executed, it allows the development team to "see" the customer response before it actually happens. It can also dramatically shorten the development process by automating routine analysis, leaving the product or service developers free to be more creative.

Customer Acquisition

Retaining and acquiring new customers is another area where the AI Factor can produce significant, measurable results. In every area of a customer's "journey" from awareness and interest through intent, action, and loyalty, AI and machine learning can enhance a company's ability to identify preferences, personalize engagement, make the conversion process easier, and facilitate repeat sales once a customer has made a purchase.[25]

Various aspects of digital marketing have gone through the Gartner "hype cycle" over the past decade, with things like customer journey analytics currently at the peak of inflated expectations. However, according to Gartner, even though AI for marketing will likely take five to ten years to reach the "plateau of productivity" for business in general, it represents significant value over the long term. Gartner's senior director analyst noted that AI-enabled technologies such as deep learning are "a marketer's most powerful way to extract insights from unstructured data and use AI to generate new content."[26]

However, companies should not wait until everyone else has embraced AI for marketing. In 2016, online gift retailer Red-Balloon had been following traditional marketing practices for fifteen years with considerable success. But it was faced with sharply rising new customer acquisition costs—from five cents to fifty dollars per customer! The marketing team was using the same SEO strategies to reach the same audiences with the same campaigns—with diminishing returns. Then, in 2017, the company deployed an AI-powered marketing platform, "Albert," that transformed the company's marketing approach, reducing customer acquisition cost by 25 percent in one month.[27]

First, RedBalloon's marketing department used the AI platform to process the company's large database of transactions and customer interactions. From that data source, it identified over 6,400 keywords to improve the search performance across the company's marketing campaigns. Then, rather than use the previous year's attribution models to inform media buys, the system would test and re-test those models in real time—to prove or disprove them—and find the most efficient way to reach the target audience. The system also identified new, high-value, and previously unknown target audiences.

By relieving marketing staff of repetitive, time-intensive tasks, such as researching keywords and manually executing search campaigns, *the AI platform freed them to do more creative and strategic campaigns*, including reaching the high-value target audiences that the AI had identified.

> The experience of using AI to identify and attract new customers revolutionized the company's digital marketing outlook. It changed their focus from "closing the deal" with a tiny percentage of their potential audience to engaging with and nurturing a far larger potential audience. This proved especially effective with social media, where the company's use of AI increased the conversion rate on Facebook campaigns by 750 percent.

Other examples of using the AI Factor (in marketing, customer acquisition, and other "power" categories) can be found in the work of NoGood, a New York-based agency founded on the idea that creativity and data science can be used to generate exponential growth. Founder and CEO Mostafa ElBermawy pointed out that traditional marketing efforts often "leave money on the table" by not being able to leverage the enormous volumes of data (structured and unstructured) that can be collected from user transactions and behaviors.

"Marketing campaigns have traditionally focused on awareness, acquisition, and activation," ElBermawy recently said. "Through the use of data science, the growth marketer gets all the way down to retention, revenue, and referral." He went on to highlight the core principle of AI-driven marketing:

"A business can forecast the customer lifetime value of new customers through the use of several machine learning and artificial intelligence methodologies." [28]

The methodology employed at NoGood is rooted in sound data science, which they apply across multiple marketing channels and disciplines.

"Every single decision we make follows scientific methods regarding data." ElBermawy said in a recent interview. "We reward scientific thinking; we don't reward luck. So every hypotheses need to be based on observation. We ask what is the metric that you're trying to move from point A to point B? How do the data support that sort of hypothesis? What is the variable you're going to change? What is your control group? What is your benchmark of success?

"Everything we do requires this understanding, whether you're dealing with a massive volume of data points when working with bigger companies, or you're dealing with a small startup that's trying to figure out product market fit. That requires us to have discipline around how we collect data, how we structure it, and how we organize and visualize the data."

ElBermawy also noted the challenges involved in *measuring* the results of AI-driven marketing. To begin with, data-driven advertising, search, and inbound marketing platforms tend to display *too much information.*

"Marketers are the target of every advertising platform on the planet," he said. "They give you a fancy dashboard and a bunch of data. Essentially, you're buying views of everything. The dashboard is fascinating and fun, but for the most part you're just getting confused. If you're not focused on one or two primary metrics for your organization, then view metrics will kill you."

Narrowing the focus of all that data to a finite number of "needle movers" is the primary role of data science when it comes to marketing initiatives. However, he also noted that it can be a combination of art and science.

"A lot of what we do is rooted in experimentation," he said. "When there are too many variables to deal with, you need to apply a macro experiment, from a statistical perspective, to reduce the number of variables you need to measure.

"But don't become so obsessed with the data that you get 'analysis paralysis.' Remember that data is a tool just like all the others that we use to make sound business decisions. It may be that data alone cannot answer a question, in which case you need to rely on experience. You need to ask questions of those who have experimented with the issue before and expand your sphere of knowledge and understanding of the problem. You should never rely on data you happen to have just because it's a 'perfect' data set."

Pricing and Costs

Another area where the power of AI solutions can be measured is in how you price your products or services and what it costs to deliver them. In chapter 5, we discussed how AI-driven cost-effectiveness is often viewed as an "optimizer" strategy often associated with well-established firms that are inherently cautious and conservative in nature. However true that may be, using the AI Factor to determine pricing and costs is a strategy that can apply to any business.

Today, there are three ways in which AI can guide companies in setting their pricing.[29] One is to more accurately lower prices on "key-value items" (those that are popular with price-sensitive customers) while also raising prices on other products to make up the difference and increase profitability.

Traditional rules of thumb for such pricing strategies can be risky. Merely matching what competitors charge or adding a fixed margin to costs is especially problematic during periods of inflation. On the other hand, AI can identify patterns and relationships between multiple products—in real time—allowing companies to discount price-sensitive products and mark up price-insensitive ones.[30] It can even allow companies to test how a slight price increase for one product would affect sales across an entire product line.

Another way AI has affected pricing is by vastly expanding the data sets used to analyze the myriad products and services available today. In addition to traditional transaction data, AI systems can parse unstructured product review and social media data from multiple sources, providing meaningful insights that would be impossible to gather manually.

According to a 2021 report by the Boston Consulting Group,[31] pricing is the most promising area for immediate application of AI solutions, in part because of the rich data environment that pricing already occupies in both B2C and B2B companies. The report, based on a global survey by MIT and the BCG Henderson Institute, indicates that once AI initiatives are applied to pricing, a company's earnings before interest, taxes, depreciation, and amortization (EBITDA) can be raised by 2 to 5 percent!

AI-based pricing initiatives are also easier for employees to accept, the report noted. Such initiatives typically provide pricing teams with user-friendly tools that require their expertise—affirming their value to the company. By freeing them from mundane, repetitive pricing tasks, AI frees them to tackle more important tasks and pursue more long-term goals. In so doing, AI-based pricing systems can pave the way for other AI initiatives where humans and technology can work together.

Just as AI has improved the pricing process, so also has it provided a more efficient workflow for predicting and planning costs. According to a white paper from the German cost management software developer FACTON,[32] AI has the potential "to minimize the risks of volatile world markets by anticipating changes that affect costs at an earlier stage." By analyzing structured and unstructured data from multiple sources, companies can anticipate supply chain changes more readily and prepare contingencies that will benefit their bottom line.

Each of these three "power categories"—product, customer, and price/cost—provides measurable results that can give companies the ability to reinvent their business models and achieve exponential growth. They can also resolve the problems, market conditions, and delivery or supply chain issues posed as the reason for using AI in the first place. Above all, they set the stage for increasing the AI Factor more broadly throughout the enterprise.

Scaling the AI Factor

Earlier, I emphasized the importance of selecting a single, high-priority AI project rather than attempting to do many of them from the start. This was not just a precaution against spreading IT resources too thin—although it was certainly a major concern. The more important reason was to prepare your business or nonprofit to scale AI and ML to accomplish even more transformational results.

In chapter 3, I described L'Oréal's "Connected Beauty Incubator" division, whose sole focus is to use data and AI to guide product development, increase business performance, and utilize smart devices in better ways. AI innovation labs are on the rise, creating "centers of excellence" for AI technology and applications. For smaller and mid-size organizations without large AI budgets, this has taken the form of "Insights-as-a-Service" entities for specific industry segments.[33]

To illustrate how one successful AI project can beget a broader, company-wide adoption of the AI Factor, I must shamelessly borrow from Jim Collins's excellent work, *Good to Great*.[34] He describes the "breakthrough moment" following the initial hard work, where you experience the benefit of built-up momentum.

For artificial intelligence and machine learning applications, the initial efforts are strenuous indeed. As outlined in chapter 7, finding the right data—in terms of sufficient quantity and quality

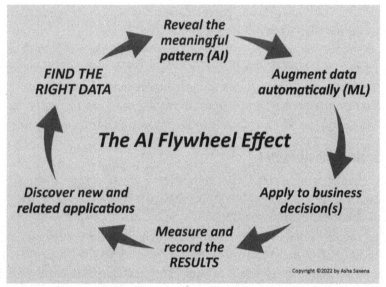

Applying AI to a broader range of new and related business activities continues the momentum of early projects to an entire organization, enabling it to reinvent itself more easily.

alone—is often challenging. But when a high-DPI project's results are measured and made widely known, more people within the company will find reasons to replicate that success, repeating the process with renewed conviction.

The benefits of scaling AI are unquestioned, but the means of doing so are less certain. In 2019, the Boston Consulting Group, explaining why seven out of every ten AI projects failed, framed the issue facing companies today. "Executives have already realized that anyone who can't find a way to use this technology at scale will be out of the game," said Sylvain Duranton, one of the consultants taking part in the study. "For this, however, it is not enough just to develop solutions: culture is needed. When an AI project is reported to the company's technology area, it is twice less likely to work than when under the command of the business area or the CEO."[35]

Strategies for scaling in many ways mirror the other processes described in this book, including anchoring the process in business objectives with C-level support, using a well-defined organizational structure and governance, and multidisciplinary, non-siloed teams.[36] Others stress the importance of starting with the best use case and "identifying which challenges you will face along the way and how to solve them."[37] Each of these checklist strategies has merit, but perhaps the best advice is to re-examine why we undertake AI-based projects in the first place.

In a 2020 article in *Harvard Business Review*,[38] authors by Athina Kanioura and Fernando Lucini proposed a radical solution—that we kill all "proof of concept" (POC) AI projects and instead launch only real-world projects, even if they begin at a smaller scale. According to their findings, companies that kill POC projects attempt to scale twice as often and end up spending less money on both pilot and fully scaled deployments. Doing so results in "nearly three times the return on their AI investments when compared to their lower-performing counterparts," according to their reporting on a survey of 1,500 C-suite executives. The authors also noted a basic flaw in using POC AI projects:

"Let's say an organization sets aside six months to build a customer experience optimization platform as a proof of concept to improve customer service. They get it up and running, confirm (as many have before) that it works, and then move it to production. Here's the mistake: they proved that a concept could technically work *without spending one hour thinking about what was needed to put it into production, the model risks, data bias, data privacy, or ethical considerations* [emphasis added]. The result? They've just put their organization into a technical debt because they never built it for scale from the beginning."

The authors go on to describe how successful AI projects can be built—when designed to solve problems in the real world. It begins with having the right structure for testing and development,[39] including the data foundation, talent, organization, and ethical framework. Such companies can skip the proof-of-concept stage altogether, create a minimum viable product (MVP), and after testing under real-world conditions, expand the project's scope.

Another factor essential to scaling AI is the growing repository of open-source code and other valuable resources, exemplified by Microsoft subsidiary GitHub. Although not entirely free from concerns over security,[40] such repositories of reusable code snippets can save AI development teams enormous amounts of time and contribute to our global knowledge of the science.

Regardless of the methods and protocols used to select, measure, and scale our AI and machine learning projects, one thing is certain. These projects will change the way we work forever.

CHAPTER 9

What Does the Future Hold?

A mere thirty-two years ago, Sir Timothy Berners-Lee published the world's first website* at the CERN nuclear research facility in Switzerland. The world wide web he began soon became the organized, interconnected, and *visual* interface for the internet—a decentralized computer network created decades earlier.†

Throughout the 1990s, this combination of interconnected, visually accessible but essentially separate, structured, and siloed data sources became what we now call "Web 1.0." It was a mirror image of the IT industry in general, where structured and isolated data silos were (and often still are) the norm. The web was simply a one-way feed—usually in the form of isolated, individual pages—of data from scattered sources to be consumed by individual users. But it was also the beginning of the phenomenon we now know as e-business.[1]

---

* If you're curious, the site can still be viewed at http://info.cern.ch/hypertext/WWW/TheProject.html.

† The web and the internet are related but *not* synonymous. The latter was a U.S. Defense Department-led initiative in the 1960s to create a distributed network of interconnected computing resources that would be less vulnerable in the event of a nuclear attack.

Throughout this book, I have been stressing the importance of transcending these isolated, decentralized data silos, exercising better data management and MDM practices. These will provide the basis for effective AI, machine learning, and more. In essence, I am advocating for companies and nonprofits to adopt the same practices that have become the norm for the past two decades—the centralization of data, ultimately to a "container" large enough to contain them, namely the cloud. During that time, our perception of what "data" means has also changed. Nontraditional unstructured data in the form of text, images, and videos have dwarfed the already large volumes of well-classified structured data that are part of every human activity. It is because of this "critical mass" of data that artificial intelligence itself becomes possible.

In the web/internet sphere, this centralization trend became colloquially known as "Web 2.0," where we not only *viewed* the data but also *interacted* with it as well. This dynamic two-way data exchange is typified by large volumes of user-generated content, social connectivity, and interactivity.[2] It is not limited to individuals sharing experiences on YouTube or Facebook, however. Businesses and nonprofits or all sizes are increasingly migrating and centralizing their on-site data operations to the cloud, under the software as a service or SaaS model. At the same time, major players like Google and Amazon were aggregating all that data for their own purposes, while also making it available as "fuel" for AI-driven projects involving social sentiment analysis, as described in chapter 6. While there is a vast economic difference between "liking" a trending video and fueling a costly, AI-driven data project, the underlying data principles are the same.

The Dangers of Centralization

While data centralization is essential to successful AI and ML projects, it also carries elements of risk. Much of the data collected and used for detecting useful patterns of behavior is monopolized by big tech companies, including Google, Meta, Amazon, and many others for their own financial gain. This is not an intrinsically bad use of data, but as discussed in chapter 4, it can lead to data being manipulated and used irresponsibly—to unduly increase financial or political power—without consent from or even against the wishes of those who provided the data.

This can have a wide range of adverse effects, from widening wealth and opportunity gaps to disenfranchisement and, in all-too-frequent cases, actual, physical harm. But as so many tragic (or merely aggravating) events have proven, merely issuing best practices mandates for data privacy and ethical/responsible data use are not sufficient. In brief:

Thoughtful, well-intentioned government or industry policies cannot stop data controllers from leveraging centralized data for their own, sometime harmful ends.

Private efforts to protect data privacy are also less than stellar. Recently, Apple made headlines by announcing changes to its app tracking transparency framework for iOS smartphones, giving users the choice of whether to allow apps to collect data rather than allow it by default.[3] Privacy advocates rejoiced, and rivals like Google and Meta were reportedly alarmed at the prospect of losing behavior-data-driven ad revenue. However, recent findings by Cornell analysts show that the measure did little to change the situation. While smaller advertisers' revenue was impacted, larger tech companies (including Apple) continue to engage in forms of tracking and invasive data practices. Their findings suggested that "while tracking individual users is more difficult now, the changes reinforce existing market power of gatekeeper companies with access to large troves of first-party data."[4]

AI and Decentralization

Fortunately, the very thing that resulted from the centralization and unification of big data—artificial intelligence—is becoming part of the solution. This is because AI is a driving force behind the phenomenon known as "Web 3.0" or "Web3."

The realities of Web3 are difficult to separate from hyperbole. Berners-Lee himself first described Web 3.0 as being focused mainly on the semantic web,[5] dealing largely with "machine-to-machine" communication. However, the concept has been widely expanded to include the decentralization of the web in general and of data applications in general.

Web3 includes many new and unfamiliar technologies, each of which requires its own book. While scores of such books are already extant, a top-level overview of Web3's "extreme decentralization" features will be especially useful to those concerned with practical AI and data applications.

The first of these, **blockchain**, is the most controversial and misunderstood, thanks to the hyperbole surrounding its most

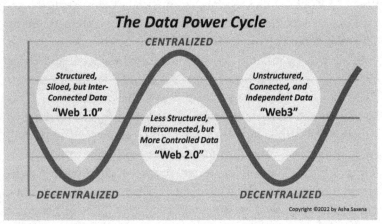

Artificial Intelligence is a catalyst for major, distributed, or decentralized technologies, including blockchain.

newsworthy byproduct, **non-fungible tokens** or NFTs. But beyond the hype, blockchain represents a fundamental shift away from centralized control of data and toward decentralized, autonomous control of one's own data. By creating an encrypted distributed transaction "ledger" for each data event, blockchain effectively cuts out the middleman, potentially providing higher accuracy and efficiency as well as theoretically greater security.[6]

While cryptocurrency and NFTs have grabbed the lion's share of the blockchain publicity, its uses are potentially more benign, as discussed in chapter 4. In its AI initiative to improve the quality of sustainably grown coffee, the owners of Coda Coffee relied on blockchain to monitor and validate the supply chain of sustainably produced beans. Other positive uses include asset transfers, self-executing contracts, and even tamper-proof voting.

Each of these Web3 developments is accompanied by others. These include decentralized autonomous organizations (DAOs), member-owned communities without centralized leadership, and the internet's potential new virtual reality (VR) interface: the metaverse.[7] While these are not all tied to AI explicitly, the emergence of Web3 should serve as a caution to companies planning a long-term AI and data strategy—since most of those companies are still firmly ensconced in Web 2.0.

From this brief summary, three things should be noted as of utmost importance for AI proponents:

- **Web3 is all about data autonomy**, giving power to the owner of the data. By decentralizing data encryption, verification, organizational structure (via DAOs), and even the way we experience people and concepts (via VR), we free ourselves from undue control and interference from traditional centers of power. While the potential for bad actors to abuse Web3 systems is very real, so is the potential for us to use data autonomy in new, productive, and beneficial ways.

- *Web3 and AI are inseparably connected.* Human beings, however talented and well-intentioned, cannot possibly manage the complexities of a decentralized, data-driven environment. (To be honest, we can barely do so in the traditional IT realm.) To move forward in a Web3 world requires a process, guided by human goals and ethics, that can simulate human decision making at great speeds—learning from the results and adjusting to meet new situations. One of those new situations, the move toward data decentralization will make things increasingly difficult for the many companies still reliant on Web 2.0 paradigms. AI can help them transition to Web3.

- *Decentralization is vital to building and scaling effective AI projects.* Chapter 8 dealt in part with the importance of applying AI and ML at scale. But as Web3 pushes us further toward decentralization and data autonomy, it will be increasingly difficult to obtain the data "fuel" that AI requires. Even with an increase in synthetic data, described in chapter 6, companies will have to become more resourceful in obtaining the right data of sufficient quality and quantity. However, companies that base their AI and machine learning projects on decentralized, Web3-based data will find it easier to scale up and achieve that "flywheel" level of momentum.

The Past Is Prologue

If your head is spinning by now, that's understandable. Even seasoned data scientists sometimes struggle to explain the complexities of these rapidly-evolving technologies or comprehend every aspect of their business value. The good news is that we've all been here before. The original "1.0" iteration of the web baffled many—until we began to see its benefits in the real world. Someday, we will look back on all this as indispensable.

Part one of this book discussed—and hopefully disproved—many of the oversimplified and misleading Hollywood notions about artificial intelligence. The AI Factor is not about robots befriending or destroying humanity. It's about how this amazing technology has the capability to help us do great things once we unlearn our fears and misunderstandings. Flaws in our own nature may lead us astray and cause harm to others. Technology can enable such harm, but it is not the cause of it. The point to remember is that:

As AI and ML are already accomplishing good things, so will related technologies like blockchain, DAOs, and even the metaverse.

Just as our fears and misunderstandings about AI prevent us from using it and using it well, misconceptions about blockchain, the metaverse, and other technologies prevent us from realizing their true potential. Today, there are admittedly acts of fraud and malice committed using these technologies. NFTs and cryptocurrency are prime examples, with the former admittedly including works that are 80 percent fraudulent.[8] Bitcoin itself is shrouded in controversy, thanks to unbridled speculation and claims that it is widely used to pay for criminal activity. (While illicit Bitcoin use has been found in the past, a recent report concluded that the criminal share of all cryptocurrency transactions had fallen to 0.34 percent in 2020.[9]) NFTs and blockchain itself are beginning to emerge as potentially beneficial to business, as they can reliably verify the authenticity of such things as service contracts and loyalty program rewards.[10]

In chapter 4, we found that blockchain (combined with AI) can have many uses besides the over-publicized ones, including recording verified transactions for good causes (sustainable farming, in the case cited) attainable by real businesses.

How We Move Forward

By now, I hope this book has provided you with a roadmap for bringing your business or nonprofit through the often-confusing world of data science—that it is your ally in achieving remarkable results. To wrap everything up, let's summarize the basic principles, rules that apply to AI and machine learning today and to newer technologies in the days to come.

- *Sustain and grow a high-achievement culture.* Building a business or nonprofit on a foundation of data science means thinking in new ways. This can be challenging for teams and their leaders, but it can also be fun and rewarding. Always make it a priority to encourage risk taking, innovative "what-if" thinking, and the recruitment of creative disruptive minds.

- *Safeguard your secret sauce.* There's a fine line between sharing general principles for the good of an industry and giving away your hard-earned techniques. When you become successful in using data to create exponential results (as you will), be careful to guard your data and methods from those who won't do the work themselves.

- *Always set new goals.* After every data-driven success, always look for the next mountain to scale. Whether you're aspiring to optimize what you're doing now, to launch a new product or service, or to disrupt everything about your current business, there are always new ways to succeed.

- **Count the cost—and the reward.** Every data project you undertake will require changes, new costs, hiring the right personnel, and choosing the right strategic partners. These will never be cheap or easy, so always hold them in one hand and the potential—but very real—benefits in the other.

- *Look for the "hidden value."* No matter what market or industry you're in, or what problem your nonprofit is tasked to overcome, things are seldom what they seem. Never be satisfied with "the way we've always done it." Look for inefficiencies and unmet needs. Ask questions. Think about problems as opportunities that data science (guided by your experience) can overcome.

- *Remember what tools really are.* Artificial intelligence, machine learning, and even technologies you think are outlandish now are powerful tools but no more. They are not magic. They only work when you know how to use them well.

Above all, don't be dissuaded by false beliefs. Popular culture is full of negative stereotypes of data science, fueled in part by its early misuse. But just as we learn to overcome the biases about AI created in movies like *Terminator* and *Her*, so too will we learn to harness the true potential of each of these new technologies—and learn to prosper with them.

Glossary of Terms

Artificial Intelligence (AI) is the core technology on which the others described in this book depend. AI leverages computers and devices to mimic the problem-solving and decision-making capabilities of the human mind. It includes a growing body of data science, including machine learning, deep neural networks, cognitive simulation, and natural language processing. It is capable of using big data effectively by facilitating autonomous decision making, problem solving, predictive and behavior analytics, and pattern recognition at very high speeds.

Big Data includes the enormous stores of existing data as well as the potential sources of data latent in any business dealing with products, services, logistics, and (of course) human activity and behavior. Big data can be characterized as having *volume* (now in the petabyte range), *velocity* (now approaching real time), and *variety* from structured data (such as tables) to complex unstructured data (such as images and video).

The Cloud, also known as fog computing or edge computing, is a metaphor for vast shared pools of configurable IT resources and services spread over multiple, connected servers. Data and applications in the cloud provide secure, on-demand, flexible, and scalable computing capabilities (for a price) to entities anywhere in the world, in support of their global and mobile operations.

Robotics and Smart Devices include a wide array of digitally controlled mechanisms that utilize artificial intelligence and big data to perform meaningful but repetitive functions. They include robots and IoT (short for the "internet of things") devices that execute repetitive or mundane tasks as well as monitor and control the production and delivery of products and services. Others include smartphones and other devices that not only collect behavioral data but also use it to influence subsequent behavior. Biometric devices serve similar functions but are actually implanted inside us to augment or enhance human capabilities.

Endnotes

Introduction

1 Lewis, Michael. *Moneyball: The Art of Winning an Unfair Game.* New York: W.W. Norton, 2011.

2 Sahota, Neil. "The AI Lords of Sports: How The SportsTech Is Changing the Business World." *Forbes*, October 25, 2020. https://tinyurl.com/yavhc7xf.

3 "What's After Terabytes and Petabytes? And when?" *Starry Blog*, July 30, 2019, https://tinyurl.com/483yytzc.

4 Houston, Peter. "Platforms Hold on to Overwhelming Share of US Digital Ad Revenue." *Spiny Trends*, November 19, 2021. https://tinyurl.com/3rbt4cdy.

5 "After Her Best Friend Died, This Programmer Created an AI Chatbot from His Texts to Talk to Him Again." *CBC Documentaries.* CBC/Radio Canada, November 17, 2021. https://tinyurl.com/58jpcysb.

6 "Millions Are Connecting with Chatbots and AI Companions like Replika." *CBS This Morning.* CBS Interactive, December 30, 2019. https://youtu.be/s2DSsrcLhFI.

7 Heikkilä, Melissa. "The Rise of AI Surveillance." *POLITICO*, May 26, 2021. https://tinyurl.com/hbz9rmx9.

8 Kraft, Amy. "Microsoft Shuts Down AI Chatbot After It Turned into a Nazi." *CBS News.* CBS Interactive Inc., March 25, 2016. https://tinyurl.com/sracvwp7.

9 Eitel-Porter, Ray, Medb Corcoran, and Patrick Connolly. "Responsible AI: From Principles to Practice." *Accenture*, March 30, 2021. https://tinyurl.com/yc43wxtj.

Chapter 1

1 Sun, Leo. "3 Top Artificial Intelligence Stocks to Buy Right Now." *The Motley Fool*, April 11, 2022. https://tinyurl.com/u7pyh94s.

2 Candelon, François, Bowen Ding, and Su Min Ha. "What do Starbucks, Tesla, and John Deere Have in Common? They've Used A.I. to Reinvent Their Businesses." *Fortune*, April 1, 2022. https://tinyurl.com/2p8k93b6.

3 Phillips, Matt, and Roberto A. Ferdman. "A Brief, Illustrated History of Blockbuster, Which Is Closing the Last of Its US Stores." *Quartz*, November 6, 2013. https://tinyurl.com/2p84wpfj.

4 Horton, Alex. "'Why Are You Still Here?': Inside the Last Blockbuster in America." *The Washington Post*, July 16, 2018. https://tinyurl.com/y8x8fkb7.

5 O'Brien, Jeffrey M. "The Netflix Effect." *Wired*, December 1, 2002. https://tinyurl.com/tp7wemem.

6 Sherman, Alex. "Expect Netflix to Keep Raising Prices." *CNBC*, November 2, 2020. https://tinyurl.com/2spwvacu.

7 Jackson, Dan. "The Netflix Prize: How a $1 Million Contest Changed Binge-Watching Forever." *Thrillist*, July 7, 2017. https://tinyurl.com/2p98yp5a.

8 "Netflix Still Mailing DVDs." *Postal Times*, June 22, 2020. https://tinyurl.com/tduvyf58.

9 Ismail, Kaya. "AI vs. Algorithms: What's the Difference?" *CMSWire*, October 26, 2018. https://tinyurl.com/2p8dkmtm.

10 Morgan, Blake. "What Is the Netflix Effect?" *Forbes*, February 19, 2019. https://tinyurl.com/4p6xnxx3.

11 Palmer, Daniel. "Starbucks: What Went Wrong?" *Australian Food News | Thought for Food*, July 31, 2008. https://tinyurl.com/5bxhx6p9.

12 Adamy, Janet. "Starbucks to Shut 500 More Stores, Cut Jobs." *The Wall Street Journal*, July 2, 2008. https://tinyurl.com/2p97dmm6.

13 Roemmele, Brian. "Why Is the Starbucks Mobile Payments App so Successful?" *Forbes*, June 13, 2014. https://tinyurl.com/4b9zzet7.

14 Ali. "Starbucks - Grinding Data." *Digital Innovation and Transformation*. Harvard Business School, April 5, 2017. https://tinyurl.com/2p9xc58v.

15 Boulton, Clint. "Starbucks' CTO Brews Personalized Experiences." *CIO Magazine*, April 1, 2016. https://tinyurl.com/4dczk4ky.

16 Rahman, Was. "Starbucks Isn't a Coffee Business-It's a Data Tech Company." *Medium*, January 16, 2020. https://tinyurl.com/yevh69js.

17 Wilson, Eric. "Starbucks, Big Data & Predictive Analytics: How Starbucks Uses Predictive Analytics and Your Loyalty Card Data." *Demand Planning*, May 29, 2018. https://tinyurl.com/5djstuxy.

18 Panko, Riley. "How Customers Use Food Delivery and Restaurant Loyalty Apps." *The Manifest*, May 15, 2018. https://tinyurl.com/ycynmf3w.

19 Oragui, David. "The Success of Starbucks App: A Case Study." *Medium*, June 12, 2018. https://tinyurl.com/zwsdycb9.

20 Marr, Bernard. "Starbucks: Using Big Data, Analytics and Artificial Intelligence to Boost Performance." *Forbes*, May 28, 2018. https://tinyurl.com/jx94j2df.

21 Grill-Goodman, Jamie. "How Starbucks Is Using Artificial Intelligence and IoT." *RIS News*, October 31, 2019. https://tinyurl.com/2p96229e.

22 Adekanye, Tosin. "Predicting Customer Churn with Machine Learning (AI)." *Medium*. Low Code for Advanced Data Science, November 12, 2021. https://tinyurl.com/5ctt9j98.

Chapter 2

1 Kendall, Graham. "Your Mobile Phone vs. Apollo 11's Guidance Computer." *RealClearScience*, July 2, 2019. https://tinyurl.com/473teext.

ENDNOTES

2   Hill, Kashmir, and Ryan Mac. "Facebook, Citing Societal Concerns, Plans to Shut Down Facial Recognition System." *The New York Times*, November 5, 2021. https://tinyurl.com/yk8tkfbd.

3   Metz, Cade. "Meet GPT-3. It Has Learned to Code (and Blog and Argue)." *The New York Times*, November 24, 2020. https://tinyurl.com/y7cps253.

4   Saunderson, Roy. "How Different Types of Analytics Tell a Different Recognition Program Story." *Authentic Recognition*, October 28, 2021. https://tinyurl.com/33nbvsm9.

5   Greenstein, Shane, Mel Martin, and Sarkis Agaian. "IBM Watson at MD Anderson Cancer Center." *Harvard Business School*, April 2021. https://tinyurl.com/2zzayadt.

6   Broussard, Meredith, and Seth Lewis. "Will AI Save Journalism - or Kill It?" *Knowledge at Wharton*. Wharton School of the University of Pennsylvania, April 9, 2019. https://tinyurl.com/2p8a7c2x.

7   Fakotakis, Nikos Dimitris. "AI Designed With a 'Sense of Smell' To Detect Illnesses from Human Breath." *Evolving Science*, September 21, 2018. https://tinyurl.com/yc5pwxhs.

8   Desmond, John. "Artificial Emotional Intelligence and Emotion AI At Work for Major Brands." *AI Trends*, June 25, 2018. https://tinyurl.com/53735sk4.

9   Siddiqui, Faiz. "Cruise Putting Driverless Cars on San Francisco Streets for First Time." *The Washington Post*, December 9, 2020. https://tinyurl.com/yckzrc5n.

10 "Big Data: The 3 Vs Explained." *Big Data LDN*, April 12, 2019. https://tinyurl.com/438cuu63.

11 Tham, Dan. "Meet Moxie, a Robot Friend Designed for Children." *CNN*, November 19, 2021. https://tinyurl.com/44r6fx9t.

12 Collins, Katie. "A Snoring Robot Labrador Puppy Stole My Whole Heart at CES 2020." *CNET*, January 8, 2020. https://tinyurl.com/5yze8hz6.

13 "Medtronic to Boost AI & Robotic Surgery Work with Digital Surgery." *Medical Devices Community*, February 19, 2020. https://tinyurl.com/53taahn2.

14 Pogue, David. "A Thermostat That's Clever, Not Clunky." *The New York Times*, November 30, 2011. https://tinyurl.com/mxw87kxt.

15 "Global Cloud Services Market Q1 2021." *Canalys*. https://tinyurl.com/2jkfr43t.

16 Keeney, Tasha. "Could a Tesla Ride-Hailing Network Run over Uber and Lyft?" *ARK Invest*, September 18, 2020. https://tinyurl.com/yaucp25s.

Chapter 3

1   Online Marketing Institute. "How Digital Marketing Crowned Domino's the King of Pizza." *Medium*. May 22, 2018. https://tinyurl.com/4748vufs.

2   Mktgbrainstorm. "Clip - Domino's Pizza at the Door of Our Harshest Critics." *YouTube*, March 19, 2011. https://tinyurl.com/3h7n587j.

3   Domino's Pizza. "Domino's® Pizza Turnaround." *YouTube*, December 21, 2009. https://tinyurl.com/2s3t353t.

4   Online Marketing Institute. "How Digital Marketing Crowned Domino's the King of Pizza." *Medium*. May 22, 2018. https://tinyurl.com/4748vufs.

5   Ignasiak, Melissa. "Domino's Launches 'The Think Oven' to Fire Up Customer Creativity." *Baer Performance Marketing*, October 26, 2012. https://tinyurl.com/2p8rwj5x.

6   Wong, Kyle. "How Domino's Transformed into an e-Commerce Powerhouse Whose Product Is Pizza." *Forbes*, January 26, 2018. https://tinyurl.com/4k2vndw2.

7   Wohl, Jessica. "Domino's Unseats Pizza Hut as Biggest Pizza Chain." *Ad Age*, February 20, 2018. https://tinyurl.com/2p9a3pv4.

8   Groysberg, Boris, Sarah L. Abbott, and Susan Seligson. "Tech with a Side of Pizza: How Domino's Rose to the Top." *Harvard Business School*, February 2021. https://tinyurl.com/ymbavs7u.

9   Dolan, Robert J. "L'Oreal of Paris: Bringing 'Class to Mass' with Plenitude." *Harvard Business School*, October 1997. https://tinyurl.com/39jjsp4t.

10 Eckfeldt, Nicole. "L'Oreal: Transforming Beauty with Technology." *Technology and Operations Management*. Harvard Business School. November 18, 2016. https://tinyurl.com/2p99tnx4.

11 Butler, Rory. "L'Oréal Powers Its R&D by Processing 50 Million Pieces of Data a Day." *The Manufacturer*, November 5, 2019. https://tinyurl.com/yx9f8c9n.

12 "The Beauty of Big Data: The L'Oréal and IBM Story." *Impact@IBMHK*. IBM Hong Kong, April 17, 2015. https://tinyurl.com/3jerwtxv.

13 Marr, Bernard. "The Amazing Ways How L'Oréal Uses Artificial Intelligence to Drive Business Performance." *Forbes*, September 6, 2019. https://tinyurl.com/bddj3zcv.

14 Roderick, Leonie. "L'Oréal on Why Artificial Intelligence Is 'a Revolution' as big as the Internet." *Marketing Week*, April 24, 2017. https://tinyurl.com/2p8cxf72.

15 RChilli Case Study. "Berkshire Associates." Accessed January 7, 2022. https://tinyurl.com/49ev6cpj.

16 RChilli Case Study. "ADP." Accessed January 7, 2022. https://tinyurl.com/2p9dt7z6.

17 No Good Case Study. "Fratelli Carli," September 17, 2021. https://tinyurl.com/5hy4smfe.

18 No Good Case Study. "Steer," October 30, 2021. https://tinyurl.com/25ncw3ev.

19 Tai, Michael Cheng-Tek. "The Impact of Artificial Intelligence on Human Society and Bioethics." *PubMed Central (PMC)*, August 14, 2020. https://tinyurl.com/yc7w8ezj.

20 Castelo, Micah. "The Future of Artificial Intelligence in Healthcare." *HealthTech*, February 26, 2020. https://tinyurl.com/3xcpm69r.

21 Chandler, Simon. "Artificial Intelligence Platform Reduces Hospital Admissions by Over 50% in Trial." *Forbes*, October 30, 2020. https://tinyurl.com/yckt3m2p.

22 Clare Medical. "Clare Medical's AI Platform Demonstrates Predictive Capabilities Which Reduced Hospital Admissions and Other Clinically Significant Outcomes by Over 50%." *PRNewswire*, October 28, 2020. https://tinyurl.com/2p8vj8y5.

23 "Hackensack University Medical Center First Hospital in New Jersey to Implement C-SATS – an AI-Powered Surgical Training Platform." *Hackensack Meridian Health*, January 9, 2020. https://tinyurl.com/2p89b52r.

24 Shih, Willy. "The Real Lessons from Kodak's Decline." *MIT Sloan Management Review*, May 20, 2016. https://tinyurl.com/yp7kk5bm.

25 Anthony, Scott D. "Kodak's Downfall Wasn't About Technology." *Harvard Business Review*, July 15, 2016. https://tinyurl.com/mumk96v6.

26 Dickinson, Mike. "Kodak to Fall from S&P 500." *Rochester Business Journal*, December 10, 2010. https://tinyurl.com/2r6eczw3.

27 "Why Kodak Failed and Netflix Didn't (A Lesson in Innovation)." *St. Bonaventure University*, August 9, 2016. https://tinyurl.com/2p84ktfe.

Chapter 4

1   Horowitz, Jeff et al. "The Facebook Files." *The Wall Street Journal*, October 1, 2021. https://tinyurl.com/bddx7pa3.

2   Swope, Peter. "Facebook Knows Its Reckoning Is at Hand—and It Isn't Ready." *Brown Political Review*, December 14, 2021. https://tinyurl.com/25wctshn.

3   Schroeder, Karisa. "3 Reasons Why Business Ethics Is Important." *School of Business & Society Blog*. University of Redlands, October 5, 2021. https://tinyurl.com/2p9d5fb3.

4   Postman, Neil. *Technopoly: The Surrender of Culture to Technology*, pp. 4–5. New York: Vintage Books, 1993.

5   Hagendorff, Thilo. "The Ethics of AI Ethics: An Evaluation of Guidelines." *Minds and Machines 30, 99-120*. Springer Link, February 1, 2020. https://link.springer.com/article/10.1007/s11023-020-09517

6   Jobin, Anna, Marcello Ienca, and Effy Vayena. "The Global Landscape of AI Ethics Guidelines." *Nature Machine Intelligence 1, 389-399*. Springer Nature, September 2, 2019. https://tinyurl.com/n4hvjfmb.

7   Gibson, Lydialyle. "Bias in Artificial Intelligence." *Harvard Magazine*, August 2, 2021. https://tinyurl.com/46cah74e.

8   Blackman, Reid. "A Practical Guide to Building Ethical AI." *Harvard Business Review*, October 15, 2020. https://tinyurl.com/ytsjbtxp.

9   Leong, Brenda, and Patrick Hall. "5 Things Lawyers Should Know About Artificial Intelligence." *ABA Journal*. American Bar Association, December 14, 2021. https://tinyurl.com/yydryfav.

10 Newman, Bradford K., ed. "Recent Developments in Artificial Intelligence Cases 2021." *Business Law Today*. American Bar Association, June 16, 2021. https://tinyurl.com/2p8nhnxw.

11 Eitel-Porter, Ray, Medb Corcoran, and Patrick Connolly. "Responsible AI: From Principles to Practice." *Accenture*, March 30, 2021. https://tinyurl.com/yc43wxtj.

12 Zaric, Gregory S., Kyle Maclean, and Jasvinder Mann. "Ethical Implications of Artificial Intelligence, Machine Learning, and Big Data." *Ivey Publishing*. Harvard Business Publishing, March 9, 2021. https://tinyurl.com/mpsdfzm6.

13 Stahl, Bernd Carsten. *Artificial Intelligence for a Better Future: An Ecosystem Perspective on the Ethics of AI and Emerging Digital Technologies*. Cham, Switzerland: SpringerLink, 2021.

14 Azoulay, Audrey, and Gabriela Ramos. "UNESCO Member States Adopt the First Ever Global Agreement on the Ethics of Artificial Intelligence." *UNESCO*, November 25, 2021. https://tinyurl.com/3hw8ax3w.

15 Hollister, Matissa. "Human-Centred Artificial Intelligence for Human Resources: A Toolkit for Human Resources Professionals." *World Economic Forum*, December 7, 2021. https://tinyurl.com/2evjjf6j.

16 Burt, Andrew. "Ethical Frameworks for AI Aren't Enough." *Harvard Business Review*, November 9, 2020. https://tinyurl.com/2sbvjhf5.

17 Horton, Melissa. "Are Business Ethics Important for Profitability?" *Investopedia*, May 27, 2021. https://tinyurl.com/237uza5c.

18 Satell, Greg, and Yassmin Abdel-Magied. "AI Fairness Isn't Just an Ethical Issue." *Harvard Business Review*, October 20, 2020. https://tinyurl.com/2p9d4dzw.

19   Gerke, Sara, Timo Minssen, and Glen Cohen. "Ethical and Legal Challenges of Artificial Intelligence-Driven Healthcare." National Library of Medicine. *PubMed Central (PMC)*, June 26, 2020. https://tinyurl.com/mry8p4by.

20   Dattner, Ben, et al. "The Legal and Ethical Implications of Using AI in Hiring." *Harvard Business Review*, April 25, 2019. https://tinyurl.com/4crwnzju.

21   Chamorro-Premuzic, Tomas, Frida Polli, and Ben Dattner. "Building Ethical AI for Talent Management." *Harvard Business Review*, November 21, 2019. https://tinyurl.com/sf332me6.

22   Fast Company Staff. "The 10 Most Innovative Companies in Data Science." *Fast Company*, March 9, 2021. https://tinyurl.com/3yz7mzda.

23   Quast, Jon, and Danny Vena. "Here's How Snowflake Is Performing Since It Went Public." *The Motley Fool*, December 16, 2021. https://tinyurl.com/4vb5kjwa.

24   Bar, Omri, *et al.* "Impact of Data on Generalization of AI for Surgical Intelligence Applications." *Scientific Reports*. Nature Research, 2020. https://tinyurl.com/y7pfzbyd.

25   Hall, Susan. "Best Friends: Harnessing Data to Save Lost Cats and Dogs." *The New Stack*, March 17, 2021. https://tinyurl.com/4tz9jvtb.

26   Youngdahl, William E., and B. Tom Hunsaker. "Coda Coffee and Bext360 Supply Chain: Machine Vision, AI, IoT, and Blockchain." *Thunderbird School of Global Management*. Harvard Business Publishing, December 1, 2018. https://tinyurl.com/5k9ujdkd.

27   McCue, Ian. "Coda Coffee Company Endures Growing Pains to Become One of Colorado's Largest Roasters." *Oracle Netsuite*, May 29, 2019. https://tinyurl.com/2p896rse.

28   Ransbotham, Sam, and Shervin Khodabandeh. "From Journalism to Jeans: Levi Strauss & Co.'s Katia Walsh (Podcast)." Me, Myself, and AI, Episode 403. *MIT Sloan Management Review*, April 5, 2022. https://tinyurl.com/ykvrw8bh.

29   Mason, Kelly. "Training Our Employees for a Digital Future." *Levi Strauss & Co*, May 17, 2021. https://tinyurl.com/36ddsj3y.

Chapter 5

1   Prajogo, Daniel. "The Relationship between Innovation and Business Performance—a Comparative Study between Manufacturing and Service Firms." *Knowledge and Process Management 30, no. 3* (August 11, 2006): 218-225. https://doi.org/10.1002/kpm.259.

2   Vardis, Harry, and Gary L. Selden. "A Report Card on Innovation: How Companies and Business Schools Are Dealing with It." *Journal of Executive Education* 7, no. 1 (2013): 15–30. https://tinyurl.com/bdzxs893.

3   Cuthbertson, Richard, Peder Inge Furseth, and Stephen J. Ezell. "Kodak and Xerox: How High Risk Aversion Kills Companies." *Innovating in a Service-Driven Economy* (2015): 166–179. Palgrave Macmillan. https://doi.org/10.1057/9781137409034_13.

4   Keeley, Larry, et al. *Ten Types of Innovation: The Discipline of Building Breakthroughs.* Hoboken, NJ: Wiley, 2013.

5   Chirio, Gino. "The 6 Ways to Grow a Company." *Harvard Business Review*, June 14, 2018. https://tinyurl.com/y4n2m59a.

6   Sedláček, Petr, and Vincent Sterk. "The Growth Potential of Startups over the Business Cycle." *American Economic Review* 107, no. 10 (October 2017): 3182–3210. https://doi.org/10.1257/aer.20141280.

7 Altman, Ian. "The Good, the Bad, and the Ugly of Cost Cutting." *Forbes*, March 17, 2015. https://tinyurl.com/24xvyjfv.

8 Gavin, Matt. "What Are Mergers & Acquisitions? 4 Key Risks." *Business Insights*. Harvard Business School, July 25, 2019. https://tinyurl.com/yckwmxew.

9 "Survey Report: Navigating the Risks of the Contemporary M&A Market." Crowe Horwath LLP, December 15, 2016. https://tinyurl.com/yzuzmacr.

10 Bonabeau, Eric. "Don't Trust Your Gut." *Harvard Business Review*, May 2003. https://tinyurl.com/3kyt2ddy.

11 Kahneman, Daniel. *Thinking, Fast and Slow*. New York: Farrar, Straus and Giroux, 2013.

12 "Data & Analytics in M&A." KPMG Australia, May 2018. https://tinyurl.com/525e4fd7.

13 Ostrowski, Sue. "How Artificial Intelligence Is Changing the Mergers and Acquisitions Process." Babst Calland Attorneys at Law, December 8, 2021. https://tinyurl.com/333uhj4z.

14 Spacey, John. "9 Types of Marketing Risk." *Simplicable*, July 13, 2017. https://tinyurl.com/452wm8z4.

15 Pappas, Nikolaos. "Marketing Strategies, Perceived Risks, and Consumer Trust in Online Buying Behaviour." *Journal of Retailing and Consumer Services* 29 (2016): 92–103. https://doi.org/10.1016/j.jretconser.2015.11.007.

16 Schuhmacher, Alexander, et al. "The Art of Virtualizing Pharma R&D." *Drug Discovery Today* 24, no. 11 (2019): 2105–7. https://doi.org/10.1016/j.drudis.2019.07.004.

17 Xing, Fei, et al. "Driving Innovation with the Application of Industrial AI in the R&D Domain." *Distributed, Ambient and Pervasive Interactions* 12203 (July 2020): 244–55. https://doi.org/10.1007/978-3-030-50344-4_18.

18 Cockburn, Iain M., Rebecca Henderson, and Scott Stern. "The Impact of Artificial Intelligence on Innovation: An Exploratory Analysis." *National Bureau of Economic Research*, May 2019. https://tinyurl.com/2p8kc5cc.

19 Elsey, Wayne. "Why Your Company Should Use AI in Hiring—but Keep It Human." *Forbes*, February 27, 2019. https://tinyurl.com/3s3d4rjk.

20 Meyer, David. "Amazon Killed an AI Recruitment System Because It Couldn't Stop the Tool from Discriminating against Women." *Fortune*, October 10, 2018. https://tinyurl.com/2p87ah9v.

21 Parikh, Nish. "Understanding Bias in AI-Enabled Hiring." *Forbes*, October 14, 2021. https://tinyurl.com/2s3ha9ph.

22 Florentine, Sharon. "How AI Is Revolutionizing Recruiting and Hiring." *CIO*, IDG Communications, September 1, 2017. https://tinyurl.com/2p83r9av.

Chapter 6

1 TNS Experts. "Data Collection: 6 Effective Methods on How to Collect Data with Examples." *The Next Scoop*, July 13, 2021. https://tinyurl.com/mryc7nps.

2 Duhigg, Charles. *The Power of Habit: Why We Do What We Do in Life and Business*. New York: Random House, 2014.

3 Reid, Andrew. "Why Your Brand Needs to Make Its (Data) Intentions Clear." *Forbes*, February 7, 2022. https://tinyurl.com/2p9avbzd.

4 Stone, Andrew. "Synthetic Data: Pharma's Next Big Thing?" *Reuters Events | Pharma*, March 22, 2022. https://tinyurl.com/4bkdn4sr.

5 Lucini, Fernando. "The Real Deal About Synthetic Data." *MIT Sloan Management Review* 63, no. 1 (Fall 2021): 1-4. https://tinyurl.com/2b96rbjr.

6 Stadler, Theresa, Bristena Oprisanu, and Carmela Troncoso. "Synthetic Data – Anonymisation Groundhog Day." *USENIX*. Accessed May 7, 2022. https://tinyurl.com/54umccbs.

7 Davis, Matt. "Top 10 Moments from Gartner's Supply Chain Executive Conference." *Gartner*, May 28, 2013. https://tinyurl.com/56j3apdh.

8 Ashford, Susan J., and James R. Detert. "Get the Boss to Buy In." *Harvard Business Review*, January-February 2015. https://tinyurl.com/4r9rzzmh.

9 Gupta, Ashutosh. "7 Key Foundations for Modern Data and Analytics Governance." *Gartner*, July 12, 2021. https://tinyurl.com/3swk5s5y.

10 "Regulation (EU) 2016/679…on the Protection of Natural Persons with Regard to the Processing of Personal Data and on the Free Movement of Such Data." *EUR-Lex*. European Union. Accessed February 23, 2022. https://tinyurl.com/3d9sayft.

11 Alizadeh, Fatemeh, et al. "GDPR-Reality Check on the Right to Access Data: Claiming and Investigating Personally Identifiable Data from Companies." *Proceedings of Mensch und Computer 2019* (September 2019): 811-4. https://doi.org/10.1145/3340764.3344913.

12 "The Battle of Artificial Intelligence: Malware vs. Antivirus." *Equinox IT Services*. Accessed May 6, 2022. https://tinyurl.com/3ebdvwdw.

13 Olson, Randal S., et al. "A System for Accessible Artificial Intelligence." *Genetic Programming Theory and Practice XV* (July 2018): 121–34. https://doi.org/10.1007/978-3-319-90512-9_8.

14 Draxl, Claudia, and Matthias Scheffler. "The NOMAD Laboratory: from Data Sharing to Artificial Intelligence." *JPhys Materials*. IOP Publishing, May 13, 2019. https://tinyurl.com/2p9ywfxk.

15 Block, Richard, and Shahid Ansari. "Spreadsheet 'Worst Practices.'" *CFO*, May 14, 2008. https://tinyurl.com/3dcyxchp.

16 Raza, Muhammad, and Stephen Watts. "Data Quality Explained: Measuring, Enforcing & Improving Data Quality." *BMC Blogs*, April 12, 2021. https://tinyurl.com/5xmpckxn.

17 Moore, Susan. "How to Create a Business Case for Data Quality Improvement." *Gartner*, June 19, 2018. https://tinyurl.com/2p82ypbr.

18 Sakpal, Manasi. "How to Improve Your Data Quality." *Gartner*, July 14, 2021. https://tinyurl.com/yckrx65c.

19 Ng, Andrew. *The Batch*. DeepLearning.AI, March 24, 2021. https://tinyurl.com/yckc4t6j.

20 "Master Data Management (MDM): What It Is and Why It Matters." *Informatica*. Accessed February 23, 2022. https://tinyurl.com/2s82hdez.

21 Sriraman, Nallan. "Master Data Eats AI for Breakfast." *Forbes*, October 7, 2020. https://tinyurl.com/yc54ds86.

22 Goyal, Sonal. "Master Data Management Eats AI for Breakfast, or Does It?" *Medium*. Towards Data Science, September 24, 2021. https://tinyurl.com/58aux9rd.

23 Everett, Dan. "How AI Improves Master Data Management (MDM)." *Informatica*, May 30, 2021. https://tinyurl.com/4sd4dap4.

24 Keskar, Harshad. "AI Driven Master Data Management." *Medium*. Tech Weekly, June 11, 2019. https://tinyurl.com/yck8cmap.

25 Tufte, Edward R. "Introduction," in *The Visual Display of Quantitative Information*, 2nd Edition, p. 9. Cheshire, CT: Graphics Press, 2001.

26 Hlandi, Marija. "What Is a Data Dashboard? Definition, Benefits, and Examples." *Databox*, June 23, 2022. https://tinyurl.com/4z3mwmuf.

27 Kenton, Will. "What Is a Bloomberg Terminal?" *Investopedia*, July 29, 2022. https://tinyurl.com/4fahpn7z.

28 Shapiro, Joel. "3 Ways Data Dashboards Can Mislead You." *Harvard Business Review*, January 13, 2017. https://tinyurl.com/5fa8s8a9.

29 Siwicki, Bill. "A CIO's Guide to AI Dashboards." *Healthcare IT News*, November 27, 2018. https://tinyurl.com/yc8pr7xd.

30 Vohra, Sanjeev and Jordan Morrow. "The Human Impact of Data Literacy." *Data Management / Accenture*, January 16, 2020. https://tinyurl.com/4xmnsm6m.

31 Brown, Sara. "How to Build Data Literacy in Your Company." *MIT Sloan*, February 9, 2021. https://tinyurl.com/2dj9wj5w.

32 Diaz, Alejandro, Kayvaun Rowshankish, and Tamim Saleh. "Why Data Culture Matters." *McKinsey Quarterly*, September 2018. https://tinyurl.com/4jv5bss5.

33 Waller, David. "10 Steps to Creating a Data-Driven Culture." *Harvard Business Review*, February 6, 2020. https://hbr.org/2020/02/10-steps-to-creating-a-data-driven-culture.

34 "Enterprise Engagement Alliance: Leading the Way to People-Centric Business." *Enterprise Engagement Alliance*. Accessed March 8, 2022. https://www.theeea.org/.

35 Bolger, Bruce. "Stakeholder Capitalism: A Primer." *Engagement Strategies Media*. Accessed March 8, 2022. https://tinyurl.com/2asj8und.

36 Gould, Scott. "Engagement Statistics," *Engagement Statistics*. January 29, 2018. https://tinyurl.com/2r739e7k.

37 Mazer, Andrew. "What Engagement Business Execs Need to Know about Analytics." *Engagement Strategies Media*. Accessed March 8, 2022. https://tinyurl.com/2pukfbk7.

38 Faria, Euler. "Learning from Experiments, a Strategy to Make Data Science Projects Scalable and Reproducible." *LinkedIn*, September 15, 2019. https://tinyurl.com/29n9entk.

39 Engler, Alex. "How Open-Source Software Shapes AI Policy." *Brookings*, August 10, 2021. https://tinyurl.com/2p9zbz77.

Chapter 7

1 Hanlon, Philomena. "The Role of Intuition in Strategic Decision Making: How Managers' Rationalize Intuition." 14th Annual Conference of the Irish Academy of Management, Dublin Institute of Technology, 2011. https://tinyurl.com/yw7waj2d.

2 Gladwell, Malcolm. *Blink: The Power of Thinking Without Thinking*. New York: Little, Brown and Company, 2005. p.23.

3 Kahneman, Daniel. *Thinking, Fast and Slow*. New York: Farrar, Straus and Giroux, 2013. p.417.

4 Marcus, Bonnie. "Intuition Is an Essential Leadership Tool." *Forbes*, September 1, 2015. https://tinyurl.com/bp77p785.

5 Davenport, Thomas H. "Big Data and the Role of Intuition." *Harvard Business Review,* June 24, 2013. https://tinyurl.com/2p9yknnz.

6 Loveman, Gary. "Diamonds in the Data Mine." *Harvard Business Review,* May 2003. https://tinyurl.com/ytkz5hpn.

7 Fedyk, Anastassia. "How to Tell If Machine Learning Can Solve Your Business Problem." *Harvard Business Review,* November 25, 2016. https://tinyurl.com/73wujm49.

8 Scalco, Dan. "6 Critical Data Points Your Sales Team Needs to Collect." *Inc.com,* April 25, 2017. https://tinyurl.com/ykx8yvf8.

9 Fontanella, Clint. "7 Call Center Metrics to Measure Your Customer Service." *HubSpot Blogs,* June 15, 2021. https://tinyurl.com/2p86j4uj.

10 Brown, Lawrence, et al. "Statistical Analysis of a Telephone Call Center." *Journal of the American Statistical Association* 100, no. 469 (2005): 36–50. https://doi.org/10.1198/016214504000001808.

11 Devillers, Laurence, Laurence Vidrascu, and Lori Lamel. "Challenges in Real-Life Emotion Annotation and Machine Learning Based Detection." *Neural Networks* 18, no. 4 (2005): 407–22. https://doi.org/10.1016/j.neunet.2005.03.007.

12 Simonite, Tom. "This Call May Be Monitored for Tone and Emotion." *Wired,* March 19, 2018. https://tinyurl.com/2p9a6eme.

13 Spacey, John. "14 Types of Market Conditions." *Simplicable,* April 11, 2018. https://tinyurl.com/2p9be2fc.

14 Szczerba, Robert J. "15 Worst Tech Predictions of All Time." *Forbes,* January 9, 2015. https://tinyurl.com/46j9369m.

15 Mimno, David, Andrew McCallum, and Gerome Miklau. "Probabilistic Representations for Integrating Unreliable Data Sources." *Association for the Advancement of Artificial Intelligence,* 2007. https://tinyurl.com/4zmrj4n.

16 "Free Public Data Sets for Analysis." *Tableau.* Accessed March 15, 2022. https://tinyurl.com/432ftxsb.

17 Pickell, Devin. "50 Best Open Data Sources Ready to Be Used Right Now." *G2 Learn-Hub,* March 15, 2019. https://tinyurl.com/22ucjypj.

18 "Public Data." *Google Public Data Explorer.* Accessed March 25, 2022. https://tinyurl.com/yc6n2hvd.

19 Mahajan, Romi. "IT Stereotypes: Time To Change." *InformationWeek,* February 4, 2015. https://tinyurl.com/54kj5vtr.

20 Reavie, Vance. "Do You Know the Difference between Data Analytics and AI Machine Learning?" *Forbes,* August 1, 2018. https://tinyurl.com/2p8vjvnw.

21 Reilly, Pete. "AI Analytics vs. Traditional Analytics: 3 Essential Differences." *Aberdeen Strategy & Research,* December 3, 2019. https://tinyurl.com/2pd9uhxr.

22 Marr, Bernard. "What Is the Difference between Artificial Intelligence and Machine Learning?" *Bernard Marr & Co,* July 15, 2021. https://tinyurl.com/5n6b3a29.

Chapter 8

1 Knopp, Evan. "Building Your AI Team: The Roles Your Enterprise Needs." *IBM, Storage,* September 17, 2018. https://tinyurl.com/bddjtv6h.

2 Stobierski, Tim. "How to Structure Your Data Analytics Team." *Business Insights.* Harvard Business School, March 9, 2021. https://tinyurl.com/2p8urx6a.

ENDNOTES

3 Moses, Barr. "How to Choose the Right Structure for Your Data Team." *Monte Carlo Data*, April 26, 2022. https://tinyurl.com/y3v26xe5.

4 RChilli Case Study. "Find out Why Berkshire Associates Chose RCHILLI's Resume Parser?" Accessed January 7, 2022. https://tinyurl.com/49ev6cpj.

5 Ng, Andrew. "How to Choose Your First AI Project." *Harvard Business Review*, February 6, 2019. https://tinyurl.com/2p8mf4nu.

6 Kahneman, Daniel. Thinking, Fast and Slow. New York: Farrar, Straus and Giroux, 2013.

7 Filmer, Joshua. "Correlation vs. Causation: The Analysis of Data." *Futurism*, November 24, 2013. https://tinyurl.com/4zrbwx59.

8 Tufte, Edward R. "The Cognitive Style of PowerPoint: Pitching Out Corrupts Within." in *Beautiful Evidence*, 159. Cheshire (Connecticut): Graphics Press, 2019.

9 Lehner, Paul Edward, et al. "Confirmation Bias in Complex Analyses." *IEEE Transactions on Systems, Man, and Cybernetics - Part A: Systems and Humans* 38, no. 3 (May 2008): 584–92. https://doi.org/10.1109/tsmca.2008.918634.

10 Rzeszucinski, Pawel. "Overcoming Confirmation Bias: An Obstacle between You and the Insight from Your Data." *Forbes*, January 19, 2022. https://tinyurl.com/2dke6at7.

11 David, Matt. "Confirmation Bias." *The Data School*, August 9, 2021. https://tinyurl.com/5hxj8c32.

12 Jobin, Anna, Marcello Ienca, and Effy Vayena. "The Global Landscape of AI Ethics Guidelines." *Nature Machine Intelligence 1 (2019): 389-99*. Springer Nature, September 2, 2019. https://tinyurl.com/n4hvjfmb.

13 Sukhadeve, Ashish. "How to Measure the Performance of Your AI/Machine Learning Platform?" *Analytics Insight*, August 29, 2020. https://tinyurl.com/mu3f222m.

14 Mattson, Peter, et al. "MLPerf Training Benchmark." *Proceedings of the 3rd MLSys Conference*, 2020. https://tinyurl.com/4aadde64.

15 Sterling, Bruce. "New Machine Learning Inference Benchmarks." *Wired*, June 26, 2019. https://tinyurl.com/bdzxdts8.

16 Linthicum, David (host) and Brijesh Singh. "AI/ML: Easier, Faster, and More Powerful with Cloud." *Deloitte On Cloud Podcast*, August 2021. https://tinyurl.com/4bs6crpb.

17 Chatterjee, Joyjit. "AI beyond Accuracy: Transparency and Scalability." *Medium*. Towards Data Science, May 13, 2020. https://tinyurl.com/464b5eu4.

18 Kesari, Ganes. "AI Accuracy Is Overrated: How Even a 'Wrong' Model Can Transform Your Business." *Forbes*, January 21, 2021. https://tinyurl.com/4jeutaus.

19 "4 Things You Need to Know about AI: Accuracy, Precision, Recall and F1 Scores." *Lawtomated*, October 10, 2019. https://tinyurl.com/2yn3ah64.

20 Columbus, Louis. "10 Ways AI Is Improving New Product Development." *Forbes*, July 9, 2020. https://tinyurl.com/3am5d8tn.

21 Wellinger, Christoph. "Digital Product Development 2025." *PwC*, April 15, 2019. https://tinyurl.com/m9j7hw8s and https://tinyurl.com/2p8ppxmj.

22 "AI Lab & Artificial Intelligence Development." *Microsoft AI*. Accessed May 7, 2022. https://tinyurl.com/2p836ezd.

23 Ehrlich, Chris. "Oracle Opens Innovation Lab in Chicago Market." *Datamation*, May 5, 2022. https://tinyurl.com/ysf8j5ev.

24 Vanian, Jonathan. "Here's One Way to Deal with the A.I. Talent Shortage." *Fortune*, April 26, 2022. https://tinyurl.com/3k2dmkbx.

25 Market Trends. "How AI Can Cut Your Customer Acquisition Costs." *Analytics Insight*, March 15, 2022. https://tinyurl.com/4kjuuc44.

26 "Gartner Identifies Six Technologies to Drive New Customer Acquisition and Growth for Digital Marketing." *Gartner*, September 1, 2021. https://tinyurl.com/t7tj2axf.

27 Sutton, Dave. "How AI Helped One Retailer Reach New Customers." *Harvard Business Review*, May 28, 2018. https://tinyurl.com/3tc7c3b7.

28 ElBermawy, Mostafa. "Data Science in Marketing: A Comprehensive Guide (with Examples)." *NoGood*, May 26, 2020. https://tinyurl.com/3afzh5mc.

29 Meyer, Anna. "3 Ways Artificial Intelligence Can Help with Pricing." *Inc.com*, June 17, 2022. https://tinyurl.com/muwr5dk8.

30 "How Companies Use AI to Set Prices." *The Economist*, March 26, 2022. https://tinyurl.com/mtvcnnrw.

31 Hazan, Joël, et al. "Why AI Transformations Should Start with Pricing." *Boston Consulting Group*, June 7 2011. https://tinyurl.com/3uxaphyz.

32 Zinser, Marcella. "Artificial Intelligence in Cost Management: FACTON Publishes White Paper on 'Predictive Costing.'" *PRWeb*, May 28, 2019. https://tinyurl.com/yu78r8n5 and https://tinyurl.com/36752hv3.

33 Aunalytics Press Release. "Aunalytics Innovation Lab Accelerates Midsize Financial Institution Business Outcomes with AI Intelligence Services." *GlobeNewswire News Room*. Aunalytics, April 12, 2022. https://tinyurl.com/mryc883m.

34 Collins, James. *Good to Great: Why Some Companies Make the Leap...and Others Don't*. London: Random House Business, 2001.

35 "Seven out of Ten Artificial Intelligence Projects Fail, According to Study." *LABS – Latin America Business Stories*, April 23, 2020. https://tinyurl.com/yucuzvjv.

36 Ribeiro, Jair. "How to Successfully Scale Your AI Project from Pilot to Production." *Medium*. Towards Data Science, February 19, 2021. https://tinyurl.com/bdebjzkd.

37 Vijay, Aabhas. "7 Proven Ways to Scale AI Projects and Speed up AI Implementation in Your Organization." *Business 2 Community*, November 29, 2021. https://tinyurl.com/5vkdsv8b.

38 Kanioura, Athina, and Fernando Lucini. "A Radical Solution to Scale AI Technology." *Harvard Business Review*, April 13, 2020. https://tinyurl.com/ydnxs3kk.

39 Lucini, Fernando. "Scaling AI for Business Value." *Accenture*, December 4, 2019. https://tinyurl.com/533uzbva.

40 Fiscutean, Andrada. "Why You Can't Trust AI-Generated Autocomplete Code to Be Secure." CSO Online. IDG Communications, March 15, 2022. https://tinyurl.com/bdzys6tk.

Chapter 9

1 Kollmann, Tobias, and Carina Lomberg. "Web 1.0, Web 2.0 and Web 3.0: The Development of E-Business." *Encyclopedia of E-Business Development and Management in the Global Economy*, 2010, 1203–10. https://doi.org/10.4018/978-1-61520-611-7.ch121.

2 The Investopedia Team. "Web 2.0 and Web 3.0." *Investopedia*, May 21, 2022. https://tinyurl.com/2p8tdntc.

3 Owen, Malcolm. "App Tracking Transparency Aimed to Solve a Problem of Apple's Creation." *AppleInsider*, March 14, 2022. https://tinyurl.com/3xyd786w.

ENDNOTES

4 Kollnig, Konrad, et al. "Goodbye Tracking? Impact of iOS App Tracking Transparency and Privacy Labels." *arXiv*. Cornell University / ACM Conference on Fairness, Accountability, and Transparency, April 7, 2022. https://doi.org/10.48550/arXiv.2204.03556.

5 "Semantic Web." World Wide Web Consortium (W3C). Accessed April 9, 2022. https://www.w3.org/standards/semanticweb/.

6 Rodeck, David and Benjamin Curry. "What Is Blockchain?" *Forbes Advisor*, April 28, 2022. https://tinyurl.com/yeytwdtb.

7 Marr, Bernard. "What Is Web3 All about? an Easy Explanation with Examples." *Forbes*. January 24, 2022. https://tinyurl.com/yc374vhu.

8 Lauer, Alex. "A Huge Portion of Our NFTs Are Fraudulent, Says Largest NFT Marketplace." *InsideHook*, January 28, 2022. https://tinyurl.com/4p93zswm.

9 Lennon, Hailey. "The False Narrative of Bitcoin's Role in Illicit Activity." *Forbes*, January 19, 2021. https://tinyurl.com/mree22wp.

10 Tasner, Michael. "Using NFTs to Grow and Fund Your Small Business." *Forbes*, March 9, 2022. https://tinyurl.com/4tskkxft.

Acknowledgments

This book was a labor of love, and the culmination of my years as a business and data champion. However, no book is a solo venture, so it's only right to acknowledge the many individuals who inspired, motivated, and assisted me in this work.

Special thanks go to my colleagues and fellow business and data professionals, many of whose accounts and case studies appear in these pages. They include Julia Bardmesser, Cameron Davies, Seth Dobrin, Mostafa ElBermawy, Jeff Garwood, Carl Gerber, Susannah Greenberg, Sowmya Gottipati, Vinay Johar, Vandana Khanna, Ellen Nielsen, Troy Sarich, Wendy St. Jude, Janneke van Geuns, and Katia Walsh.

I would also like to thank my fellow members of Women Leaders in Data and AI, whose support and enthusiasm feeds my soul and fires my imagination each and every day. These include board members Michael Kingston, Ellen Nielsen, Seth Dobrin, Scott Mordell, Dara Meath, Tracy Ring, Isabel Gomez Garcia de Soria, and Tina Rosario. I must also thank WLDA's corporate sponsors Accenture (Jack Azagury), Alteryx (Libby Duane Adams and Paula Hansen), Chevron, Deloitte, L'Oréal, and Molex, as well as advisors Kevin Adams, Katy Davis, Steve Fleischner, Jeffrey Garwood, and Clifford Schorer.

Other WLDA members include Adita Karkera, Alexandra Ross, Andrea Markstrom, Ann Josephine Flanagan, Besa Bauta, Bharti Rai, Bhavna Mehta, Brenda Fiala, Cameron Davies, Carl Gerber, Carrie Cobb, Chitra Narasimhachari, Cindi Howson, Claus Torp Jensen, Danielle Crop, Dara Meath, Dena Bellack, Diane Schmidt, Eileen Vidrine, Elfijie Lemaitre, Elizabeth Cook, Ellen Nielsen, Erin Stanton, Gabriela de Queiros, Jacqui Van der Leij-Greyling, Jalaine Ulsh, Jan Choy, Janneke van Geuns, Jennifer Schultz, Joy Mimum, Julia Bardmesser, Kalyani Boddupalli, Kamaljeet Ghotra, Kamayini Kaul, Karen Evans, Kash Patel, Kendra Burgess, Kevin Adams, Lynette Kenney, Lynda Alleyne, Madeline Leone, Marcus Daley, Margery Connor, Maria Nazareth, Maria Villar, Maria Voreh, Mayanka Melville, Megan Meinen, Meghan Anzelc, Melanie Brown, Melanie Johnsen, Melissa Drew, Michael Kabella, Michael Kingston, Michelle Dunivan, Michelle Pooser, Michol Porter, Mike Giresi, Naveen Khan, Nicki Halle, Nisha Patel, Peggy Plogh, Peggy Tsai, Pinkrose Hamilton, Rachel Richter, Rosemary Walsh, Samta Kapoor, Sandy Carter, Seth Dobrin, Sherry Marcus, Stephanie Perrone Goldstein, Sowmya Gottipati, Susannah Greenberg, Tamara Uvaydov, Tami Frankenfield, Tammy Roust, Tealisha Williams, Tina Rosario, Tracy Ring, Wendy Lawhead, and Yuqing Sun.

Special thanks to my colleagues on the CEO Coaching team: Mark Moses, Jason Reid, Sheldon Harris, Don Schiavone, Jerry Swain, Jim Weaver, Chris Larkins, Craig Coleman, Cynthia Cleveland, Davis Sobek, Emily Murphy, Gerry Perkel, Jacquie Hart, Jamie Cohen, Jim Weaver, Kevin Adams, Lew Jaffe, Michael Klaus, Michael Marchi, Mike Morris, Odmar Almeida-Filho, Pascal Brochier, Phill Sullivan, Rafe Wilkinson, Ramona Cappello, Shep Moyle, Steve Sandusky, Tracy Tolbert, Rachel Smith, Sean Magennis, and Heidi Smith.

I had the able assistance of many skilled people in this publishing venture. They include John Parsons, my editor and collaborator, Jill Marsal, my literary agent, and Heather King and her magnificent team at Post Hill Press.

Most of all, I want to thank my wonderful sons, Milan and Siddharth Saxena, for all their love and support.

About the Author

Currently an Adjunct Professor of Health Policy and Management at Columbia University, Asha Saxena is a strategic innovative leader with a proven track record of building successful businesses, a strong academic background, creative problem-solving skills, and a clear vision for guiding businesses to growth and success.

Asha has served as Entrepreneur-in-Residence for Columbia Business School and is on the faculty of Columbia University, Mailman School of Public Health. She teaches healthcare consulting, entrepreneurship, Big Data, and data analytics courses to MHA, MPA, MBA, and EMBA students and is a keynote speaker on Big Data. She graduated from Southern Methodist University with an MS in Data Science and an undergraduate degree in Computer Science Engineering.

One of Asha's most recent accomplishments is the founding of Women Leaders in Data and AI (WLDA), a mastermind networking group for women leaders in the tech world that offers peer support, industry expert–hosted events, workshops, and guidance on leadership development. WLDA founding members include women leaders at organizations like the FBI, TD Bank, Chevron, Amazon, the *New York Times*, Merck, and Cigna.

Asha also served as a CEO of Aculyst, Inc., a healthcare analytics firm. Prior to that she served as a President and CEO of Future Technologies, Inc. (FTI), an international data firm specializing in data analytics solutions for Fortune 1000 companies in the US.

In the area of operational excellence, Professor Saxena is certified as a Six Sigma Black Belt professional. She started her professional career in a New York-based IT firm and has enjoyed challenging, diverse assignments in the financial services industry. She was invited to be a part of the World Economic Forum, where Future Technologies Inc. was named a "Global Growth Company 2007." She has also enjoyed success as a restaurateur, real estate developer, movie producer, and contributor to *Entrepreneur* magazine.